B. OR B.O.S.S.

A FEMALE ENTREPRENEURS GUIDE TO SHOWING UP FOR THEIR CUSTOMERS LIKE A B.O.S.S.

By

JENNICA ANDERSON

B.I.T.C.H. OR B.O.S.S.

www.servicecoachingwithjennica.com

ISBN: 979-8-9866664-2-6

Dedication Page

To My Heavenly Father, thank you for ordering my steps through this process and never leaving me nor forsaking me.

Table of Contents

To all female business owners out there, this is for you. This is your how to be the bigger person manual as well as your how to be you in your business while establishing boundaries and maintaining professionalism with your customers. Contrary to what we have been taught in corporate America, it is important to know there is more than one way to lead. You don't have to be stuck up and overly aggressive. You can be exactly who you are just an enhanced version. In corporate America, I was always told by people who barely knew me that they didn't think I was assertive enough for leadership because I smile and laugh often but the more knowledge I obtained and experience I got, the more comfortable I was standing in my place as a transformational leader with the ability to change styles as necessary. The more I heard it, the more it annoyed me. I grew unapologetic in my ability to lead and quite frankly didn't care what other leaders thought. The results were evident, and I felt good about developing others without belittling them or being a bitch. Leadership has never been about power to me, it has always and will always be about transforming others into the best version of themselves. I want to be a leader that values and embraces every leadership style. I try to be an example of what making a conscious choice to lead by example, smile and be positive looks like. The term B.O.S.S. in this book

1

refers to a Business Owner Showing Superintendence. It is about being professional at all times, even when it gets hard. It is about being a leader above all and not compromising that for anything or anyone. Most importantly, it is about being the absolute best version of you for your customers each and every day.

INTRODUCTION

I have a goddess passion for service and have had it for literally most of my life! I am an imperfect follower of God that loves all people and have devoted my life to helping small business owners maximize their customer experience and transform the way they show up for their customers. My first job wasn't your normal fast-food job, grocery store, or wherever most people's first job was. My first job was a customer service agent in the summer. My mom was a corporate trainer, so she got it for me and made the service expectation clear. In my younger days I was always smiling, super nice and wanting to help someone, I quickly identified my natural personality was perfect for customer service. I was able to control the tone of all of my calls because my personality was contagious and at 16, that was a big deal to my supervisors but to me I was just running my mouth, having fun and being me.

Fast forward to when I graduated high school; I was pregnant and beginning college, I started at a Fortune 500 company in another call center and rose to leadership within 2 years, just being me. I took a break from school because life and babies happened, but I was still able to progress in my career. When I started in leadership, I realized my always nice and giggly personality did not always work when I was coaching other people because everyone wasn't like me; the ability to be kind and a natural problem solver was not as natural for everyone else as it was for me and being nice alone didn't make me a good leader. I was personally aware but not so much aware of others and how they learn. The very things that made me great as an entry level complicated my path to leadership and although I didn't understand it, I didn't get discouraged. At first, I struggled with imposter syndrome, and I tried to do things the way I saw other leaders do it and it was a total shit show at first. When I was too serious everyone constantly asked if I was okay. When I joked too much some took it personally. When I was too relatable, I had to work twice as hard to get agents to know when to be serious. When I was direct, I am pretty sure my reps called me a bitch behind my back (like 100% sure).

It was obvious, I had to find my own approach. I began investing in developing my leadership skills and understanding different kinds of people through classes at school, books, seminars, webinars, workshops and whatever else I could do to learn more about leading different kinds of people. The more I learned about myself, the more I learned about others. Who would have thought there was a leadership style for people like me? My dedication to seeking knowledge and constant improvement allowed me to become a great leader and develop customer service skills in others, by helping them leverage their own personality. Does that mean I take myself too seriously or I changed the silly personality that makes me who I am? Absolutely not! I tried and I can't be the person that takes themselves too seriously, it just makes people weird and fake around you.

I am a bubbly personality; I smile *A LOT* and my ability to meet people where they are and encourage authentic development makes me feel more pride than having people afraid of me or compromising my morals and ethics at the recommendation of other leaders. I thought for so long there was only one way to lead and get things accomplished and that was such bullshit. As women, in corporate America, we are always placed in situations that require us to suppress how we feel or who we are in order to accommodate the expectations of others. There is nothing wrong with who you are. Whether you are silly, bossy, a pushover, or possessive, I am here to tell you there is a leader in you. When you work for someone else, very seldomly are multiple leadership styles accepted or taught, unless you worked for a really great company with an awesome executive leadership team. As your own B.O.S.S, you get the chance to step into your own version of being a B.O.S.S. and lead in a style that comes natural to you. I believe God will lead you to lead others through the calling he has on your life. Being a business owner is a leadership role, rather you were ready for it or not. Ownership requires leadership, *NO EXCEPTIONS.* It requires professionalism and elevation.

I bet you are wondering but how do I do that in the business I am in? The answer is quite easy, through your customers and employees. In this book, I am going to help you figure out what your primary leadership style is and how to use it to best service your customers. Marketing experts will tell you your brand reflects your personality and that is absolutely true BUT no one ever told you the rest. Let me, your customer service and management skills should reflect your leadership style. The way you lead should be in alignment with who you are, what you value and what your employees need. Do you know what kind of leader you are? Do you know how to use that to best service your customers and your employees? If not, that is fine because I am going to walk you through it, by the end of this book you will discover a lot about yourself, your primary leadership style and what that means for your customer service. This book will be a wealth of information and I will give it to you, my way. If you are looking for a book so serious that you will never laugh aloud or feel like I am coming directly for you this may not be the book for you but know there is a method behind my madness and change happens when you get a little uncomfortable.

I am going to give you the tools to B.O.S.S. up and transform your brand's customer service by revealing the strengths and skills you already have in you and changing the way you view leadership! This book will challenge you to dig deep within and bring forth who you are capable of being for your customers. As you put the things you learn in this book into practice, remember this, you want to be a leader in customer service in your industry. You don't just want to do the minimum and be average but be the BEST! It is not easy, or everyone would be equal and that is just not the case. How many Chick Fil A competitors are there? Exactly! Everyone is capable but not everyone is really to rise to this level of leadership. Always being a leader for your brand will require some rising because let's face it some people are just difficult to interact with but after reading this book, you will rise to the occasion with a smile on your face when faced with adversity and vulnerability.

Vulnerability is a big part of being a great leader, but you will need to be vulnerable with the right people at the right times, not your cheer leaders or yes men/women, I like to call them. You know not the ones that say things like, "girl, I would have done the same thing" or will encourage you to do what you know you shouldn't. You want to be vulnerable with someone that will challenge you to B.O.S.S. up and be your best; if you don't have someone like that don't worry, I got you! Join our community for resources and a link to our Facebook group at www.bitchorboss.org. It is my goal, that after reading this book you feel liberated and inspired to show up every day for your brand like a B.O.S.S. in your own way.

CHAPTER 1

WHICH B ARE YOU?

"She may be a bitch, but she's a genuine bitch with a good heart."

~Emily Henry

When you were younger do you remember when your superintendent came to the school? I mean everyone was on their best behavior, principle included. Every superintendent I ever encountered just had a presence of professionalism and business and they demanded that of others, from students to parents to teachers, just with their position of authority and the way they carried themselves at all times. Not saying they were the nicest people, but we didn't know, we just knew they were serious. Their title didn't stop parents from disagreeing with their decisions or giving them an ear full at board meetings, but they knew where not to cross the line when it came to the superintendent and the person making the decisions, not because they were going to be rude and disrespectful in return but because they held a position of authority and stature. Respect was expected without being requested.

This is how you should show up for your business every single day. Like a B.O.S.S.! No matter the size of your business, you are the CEO, and you should show up every day as such. It won't stop your customers from ever being upset with you, but it can certainly change how they approach your brand with their dissatisfaction. Everyone has potential to be a Business Owner Showing Superintendence (B.O.S.S.) but that takes a lot of skill and practice. A B.O.S.S. knows themselves as a person and is a conscious leader. A B.O.S.S. is someone who understands their position in their business, their customers, and the customer experience; but what if you can't? What if you know nothing of leadership and the customer experience? The truth? If you are unable to show up to your brand as the leader you are, you are indeed a Boss Imposter Trying to Cover Herself (B.I.T.C.H.). Relax, I'm not calling you an actual bitch, it is an acronym; I am just saying you are not showing up how you should be you are pretending to be something you haven't done the work to become. By imposter I mean just that someone pretending to be something they are not to deceive others, which is different than imposter syndrome. One is focused on the perception of others and the latter is focused on the perception of self. People know how you show up for your brand and they may even return a few times when you are showing up really crappy but having a good product or service will only sell itself for so long.

Customers will grow inpatient of poor service and move on to a competitor when they reach their breaking point. Loyalty is earned not owed and I hate to tell you but having great products is not enough to create an emotional loyalty with your customers. You are going to have to learn to understand the emotions of others and dig into your strengths and weaknesses in order to show up like a B.O.S.S. for your business every day, in every way and in every situation.

I highly recommend the book, "Emotional Intelligence 2.0" by Travis Bradberry and Jean Greaves for a thorough introduction to emotional intelligence. That is the great part about Emotional Intelligence (EQ), it can be improved with conscious effort, so if you have a really difficult time understanding your customers and where they are coming from, all hope is not lost. It will take work, but your EQ can improve if you are committed to it. The logic and development of what makes a good leader is extremely subjective. Some people believe not everyone is capable of being a good leader and I whole heartedly disagree. I believe anyone who is committed to understanding and improving EQ has the capability of being a leader and B.O.S.S. I know there are some small business owners that come from successful leadership positions and are showing up as a B.O.S.S. every day for their brand, but most of the time that is not the case for self-made small business owners.

So which B are you? Some owners are complacent with limiting their customer base to those who are willing to accept mediocre service and lack of leadership. Sometimes reality shows us a need for change, sometimes it doesn't. It is not because the learning opportunity isn't there; it is because we are too busy being a B.I.T.C.H and only looking at the limited income doing the bare minimum is bringing in, instead of evolving and thinking about how far our brand could go if we stopped pretending and actually start showing up like a B.O.S.S. in real life. When pretending, there will always be a limit to how far your business can go because not every consumer will deal with a lack of willingness to improve, inexperience and excuses. I have been doing this a while and I already know some of you reading this book are having trouble determining where you fall or you may be giving yourself a little more credit than you should because you are making sales or booking clients and no one has complained, but the truth is when you know and understand your customers, your customer experience, and yourself as a leader, you will be able to call yourself a B.O.S.S. with no doubt or hesitation because customers have told you and they shared it with their friends. Let's take a look at the not so obvious and decide where you really fall.

The customer experience refers to the end to end experience a customer has with your brand and how it makes them feel, both subconsciously and consciously. When there are pain points in the customer experience, or things that can cause customer abrasion, customer service becomes necessary. The customer service factor in the customer experience refers to how you are able to help a customer throughout their journey with your brand. So, if you are one of the; I don't answer questions because it is on the website business owners, keep reading because this book is no doubt for you! If you are not helping, you can't think you are providing good customer service, can you? If customer service is provided professionally, thoroughly, and kindly it can win a customer by itself. Customer service is what creates emotional loyalty and allows relationships and trust to be built between your customers and your brand. The outcome of customer outreach eventually results in either separation or commitment to your brand. Customer service satisfaction can vary based on your mannerism when you respond to an inquiry, this can be your professionalism, this can be your communication timeframe, how well you explain your product/service, and this can be your problem-solving skills or lack of. This is how you responded to the lost package, how you followed through or up, how you right your wrongs, or your appreciation and retention effort. There is no way of pretending with this factor. Either you are a B.O.S.S. or you are pretending to be and most often you are not doing a good job pretending because your frustration easily protrudes through the facade of professionalism and superintendence.

Can you say that when customers interact with you that you are showing up like the superintendent from grade school or like the CEO of a multi-million-dollar company? Not just when it is easy but when you get the customer who always wants something free, the one who is upset because the postal service lost their order in transit, the one who never gets their order that shows delivered, the one who thinks the louder she screams the more you hear, the one that is calling after you performed a service they confirmed they were pleased with to say they weren't pleased and want a refund, or my favorite the customer with one million questions. Most people think it is impossible to be nice when you are faced with such difficult situations and different kinds of people but it's not and it's also not about the customer being right. It is about the customer feeling heard and you showing up like a B.O.S.S. because that is your position and not allowing anything less of yourself. Being a B.O.S.S. is hard work, trust me, I know, but it is possible to show up every day like a B.O.S.S. for your customers and employees. To be a great leader you have to learn to be a great servant and have a great deal of personal awareness. I have created an assessment for you to complete that will give you more insight on your primary leadership style as it relates to the examples in this book specifically. If you have not already done so, visit our membership site created for this book, www.bitchorboss.org , and take the assessment before moving on to chapter two, in which we will look at a few common types of business owners and their leadership styles.

CHAPTER 2

THE RUDE BUSINESS OWNER

"Please bore someone else with your questions, that's all."

~ Amanda Presley

Devil Wears Prada

Have you been called rude and unprofessional more often than you would prefer, and you don't understand why, or you think it is the customers fault because they don't read, they ask too many questions or any other reason? Well, this one's for you! The rude business owner is often easily annoyed and unnecessarily cold. Rude to a customer is often direct to this business owner. The rude business owner is typically an autocratic leader, primarily. Autocratic leaders tend to be more aggressive leaders. They are direct, to the point, stubborn and even bossy. Power is important to this type of business owner.

Have you ever worked for a manager that walked around barking orders and power tripping for no reason? I am willing to bet they were autocratic leaders. Autocratic leaders rely heavily on their position of power and seldomly interact with those that are beneath them.

You will find a few business owners that are not anything like described but they still act like they can't help customers/clients because they have made the information accessible and those are not true autocratic leaders, these are more than likely a different kind of leader that either doesn't want to do the work or has been taught by a more established autocratic leader this is how they should act. Autocratic leaders often leave little room for flexibility in their business. Autocratic leaders tend to have trouble looking at things from different perspectives and taking advice from others, so if this is you, I would imagine you are rolling your eyes at this book already, but it is ok we are going to get through this together! I promise you; I am an expert in customer experience and customer service. Autocratic leadership is one of the least effective leadership styles, with both customers and employees, but it is not all bad.

Autocratic leadership is the most effective type of leadership style when dealing with stubborn, inexperienced, or uneducated staff. This leadership style has an amazing ability to create an obedient environment and get results. So, if none of what I said screams you, but you are a little late to the leadership party and you already have staff members just doing whatever they want, I would encourage you to explore this type of leadership for yourself or look for an office manager with this primary leadership style. If you need to adopt this style to whip your employees in shape, make sure you use it in moderation. Although an autocratic leader can thrive in a weak environment of inexperienced people, this type of leadership can destroy the morale of a team and make team members not feel valued. My favorite autocratic leader is, Miranda Priestly, in the film, "The Devil Wears Prada." She was a total badass and very to the point, but can you imagine if she had to talk to customers after how she treated her staff? In the film when she said, "truth is, no one can do what I do." That summed up autocratic leadership in the workplace. They usually feel like it has to be their way or the highway. This leadership style is the most difficult to work for and have when dealing with customers. They seldom value the opinion of others. If autocratic leadership is your primary leadership style, I will be honest you will require the most transformation when servicing your customers but nothing that I can't help you with. Let's take a look at some of the traits of an autocratic leader and how you can use them to show up for your customers like a B.O.S.S.

Quick Decision Making

Being able to make decisions quickly is great in a high stress situation but when dealing with customers it can cause you to be impulsive and not think about how what you say or do will impact others or your business for that matter. In order to prevent overly blunt responses, it is important you utilize quick response templates for written communication. Quick responses are detailed responses to frequently asked questions that you have readily available for customer interactions to just copy and paste, or read, if needed. I would include a detailed description of all the products and services you offer. I know you like to refer customers to the source you see fit but they are not your employees, they don't work for you. It is not your job to make them independent learners, you are just creating pains in their customer journey and each time you do that you are missing an opportunity to create a moment of delight and build an emotional relationship with your customer. Emotional relationships foster long term customer loyalty. The key is completing your quick responses BEFORE you are placed in the situation. Most people would have trouble thinking of questions but due to your enthusiastic personality and instinct, I would imagine this will come easy to you. Visit (www.bitchorboss.org) for a start to your quick responses.

Lack of Empathy

This leadership style is usually very knowledgeable, the lowest on the EQ scale and higher on the IQ scale. We will discuss a few ways to improve your EQ with this leadership style later on in this chapter but for now, while you are still learning you have to ask your customers. Since you have the natural God given ability to produce solutions and make decisions it is imperative you send your customers detailed surveys regularly. You need to ask specific questions and get suggestions to guide you in process and experience modification. For example, you want to ask a customer how they would rate their experience with your brand & how customer experience can be improved. Once you have answers, decide if making the suggested improvements are feasible and do they have a return on investment (ROI)? If so, decide could other customers benefit from the changes? If not, what can you do to ease the specific customer concern within your ability?

Now, when new issues arise in real time that is when things usually go left for this type of leader, but it is cool you will be prepared, verbally go through the steps we just talked about. Ask customers the same questions and go through the same series of questions to yourself to get resolution. You can also use those series of questions when responding to reviews. When responding to issues, reviews or feedback remember these three things:

➢ *Apologize*

➢ *Acknowledge*

➢ *Resolve*

Apologize for how it was perceived, acknowledge customer concerns and/or emotions, and resolve by letting them know what you produced in your series of questions to yourself. An example would look something like this, a customer is upset about how they were treated when they came into your store so they go to a review site and give you one star and start talking about how they weren't helped when they came in, no one spoke, they were in line too long and the cashier was rude.

First off, count to ten because I know you like to tussle... not literally but this leadership style is enthusiastic and will be quick to respond. When you are impulsive your response to any conflict is to defend and defending is simply a reaction. As a B.O.S.S. you don't react, because it gets you nowhere but a more escalated situation, instead you respond and resolve. *Acknowledge, Apologize and Resolve*. Your response could be something like, "I apologize for this less than anticipated experience with our store. I understand how that can be frustrating, it is never our intention to make customers feel unvalued. We want all of our customers to enjoy their experience with us. Please be advised we have sent our cashiers through extensive customer service training to better handle stress in the workplace and customer service soft skills. We hope that you will visit us again and allow us the opportunity to improve your perception of our establishment. We value your feedback, and we value you as a customer."

Rule Driven

Rules are necessary especially when you have problematic employees but that makes it even more important to make sure your policies are created with your ideal customer in mind. If you want customers to follow the policies, make ones that won't piss them off.... well, most of them. Create policies that make your brand easy to do business with for your ideal customer and that will significantly reduce the chances of being asked to bend any rules. You are a stickler for processes and rules but that can set you up for failure when you make them based on what you want and not your customers. I would really suggest hiring a CX consultant to plan and blueprint this for you, as this leadership style has the most difficulty putting themselves in other's shoes. If that is not in the cards right now, I get it. Visit the complimentary site for this book and download the customer experience workbook to help establish your customer personas and customer centric policies. Once you establish policies, place them at all of your awareness touch points, social media, google, website, etc., pretty much where a customer can find your brand.

Bossy

Believe it or not, this is not a bad thing. As an autocratic leader you have an innate ability to make sure employees know exactly what they should be doing and how in order to accomplish a task. You can do the exact same thing for customers. Instead of using this trait as an excuse to just give short answers or links, give customers everything they need to accomplish the ultimate task, which is to make a purchase. You are indeed responsible for educating customers on your products and/or services (after all you are the expert, right?!) and the number of followers you have or the quality of your work/products does not give you the right to be rude or justify a lack of customer service, as a business owner. All questions do dignify an answer. Autocratic leaders are usually skilled and passionate leaders. They have the information to persuade the buyer, so give it to them. No customer has ever complained about getting too much info.

This authoritarian type of leadership style is not like any other so if this is you, you know it and it is important to live in your truth. This personal awareness will allow you to move with intention when dealing with your customers and hiring employees. If you just discovered this is your primary leadership style, it is important you work on your EQ before you begin hiring employees because you don't want high value employees to leave because you don't make them feel like you appreciate the value they bring. If you already have employees, now worries you will just need to work on your EQ while applying what you have learned at the same time. Here are a few tips on improving your ability to deal with customers as an autocratic leader:

1. Get a Journal- In order to be mindful of others you must be aware of yourself. You have to understand your feelings. Get a journal and write down how you feel and why you feel the way you do. (You can visit the book website for an e journal)

2. Ask questions and listen- It will more than likely always be more of a challenge for you to have empathy, so ask questions. Inquiring shows you care and gives you the opportunity to listen to how others feel. This should improve your ability to be empathetic and be less defensive.

3. Be patient, don't interrupt-You can't always react, resisting the urge to react and defend will teach you to be more responsive and less reactive

4. Empathize- Put yourself in the shows of others and try to see things from their point of view

CHAPTER 3

THE PASSIVE & NON-CONFRONTATIONAL BUSINESS OWNER

"Never be too busy to not think of others"

~Mother Teresa

U nlike the leadership style in the previous chapter, not all leaders are about control and self, in fact, quite the contrary; most other leadership styles have different motives. Passive and non-confrontational people are typically introverted, timid, spiritual, and/or religious. Although, being this type of person can be beneficial, when it is not practiced sparingly and strategically, it can be confused for weakness and that can cause great issues in life and in your business. According to Webster Dictionary, passive is, "not to take an active or dominant part." Passive and non-confrontational leaders tend to err on the side of caution for a variety of reasons including everything is often left to fate. They want to keep the peace; they want their religion to be reflected in the way they run their business and plenty of other reasons.

All of the reasons listed make a great foundation of a servant leader. Servant Leadership is a leadership about serving instead of power and authority. Servant leaders focuses on people first. It focuses on interacting with and serving the needs of others in order to reach success. Servant leadership is the most selfless form of leadership and actually extremely effective in most situations. Without proper practice natural born servant leaders can seem weak and like pushovers and if you allow customers to walk all over you that will ruin your business. Why is it that most servant leaders fail in entrepreneurship? Because in efforts to serve the needs of others they fail to serve the needs of all, which includes the company. Let's put it into perspective, many companies practice servant leadership at a very high scale and achieve great success, my two favorite companies that practice servant leadership are Chick-Fil-A and Starbucks.

The core values are different but servant leadership is the core of the business. These two examples show you don't have to be religious to be a servant leader. Although servant leadership is described throughout most religious teachings it certainly is not restricted to just the ultra-religious persons or religious based businesses. Servant leadership is for any person or business that wants to be committed to serving others (both customers and employees). My all-time favorite example of a servant leader is, my Disney homegirl, Mulan. Yes, Mulan was a servant leader. There have been many amazing servant leaders, such as Mother Teresa but I am a realist and Mulan is such a practical example.

I am a big Disney junkie in cinema and customer experience. Mulan secretly went to the army in her father's place and becomes a hero that leads the Chinese army to great victory. She didn't do it for herself, she did it for those around her and for the success of her country. She didn't just go with the flow when she wasn't doing well and chalk it up to destiny; instead, she practiced the three P's: Patience, Perseverance, and Persistence. She started out passive and turned into a Bad ass servant leader as will you if you utilize your strengths to your advantage with both your employees and customers. Let's take a look at natural traits of servant leaders and how you can use them to serve your customers and employees without allowing them to run over you and you continue making profit.

Positivity

I believe in the power of a smile and positive words and you are naturally great at that. That doesn't mean you can't say no and be positive. It is important you leverage your positivity without using it as a crutch. Your desire for positivity at all times should not cloud your judgement when delivery bad news or news in which you expect some push and dissatisfaction. You just reposition your positivity, this is called indirect organization of a message. You present your logic and reasoning first, and then deliver the primary message. For example, "We try our best to provide the highest quality products we can at affordable rates for our customers and in order to that we are unable to discount our products. You are able to join our email list and we can notify you when we have our yearly sales. You won't want to miss out on those!" It is also important you know the different in tone and style when communicate. You are a positive person so I'm sure your tone is always positive but your style refers to your words and language in communication and it is important that you don't follow my tip above but use words that show you are comfortable with your choice such as unfortunately when it not is unfortunate, lol when you aren't laughing or I am sorry when you have nothing to be sorry for.

Giving

Servant leaders are extremely selfless. Giving kind of goes with positive but it is still a little different. They put the needs and desires of others above themselves. In customer experience design business goals meet customer needs. It is important for you to ask for customer feedback regularly. Although you may not be able to please all you will get relief in knowing you are pleasing most in their customer journey. Create hours, prices and policies with your ideal market personas in mind and stick to them. I would encourage you to establish escalation procedures for different scenarios, so you have levels to work around before you do what the customer requests. You may not be able to do what customers/ employees want but focus on what you can do to make them feel valued and heard. It is important for you to be ok with the fact everyone won't be able to afford you and that is ok, you will be right there waiting for them when they can.

We can expand products and services for different budgets but we cannot discount our products and services to accommodate people who just don't' have it. Lastly, a B2C relationship is just that a relationship, just like an intimate relationship you can't fall in love with potential in business you can't want to help someone because you see there potential. I speak from experience you will get no were but very irritated giving others free game waiting for the moment they decide to pay you because they see your value and their potential. It will never happen so save your brain cells, energy and time by focusing on who your target customer is and letting those with potential know confidently and nicely you will be right there ready to create magic when they are ready.

Community Driven

A lot of non-profit business owners are servant leaders because of their commitment to community improvement. Whether you are for profit or non-profit community is a great way to build trust, relationships and profit when done strategically. When one is community driven it is natural to think you have to please your community of customers at all times by any means necessary but that is not practical and will not help your customers take you seriously. When you hear the customer is always right. It is true, but not how you think. This phrase means the customer always has the right to feel how they feel. In order to make that phrase true to you without giving everyone everything they desire you create a sense of community and source for feedback. Invest your time into building a community in which customers can talk and give feedback. Encourage collaboration and engagement. You can do that via social media websites, blogs, or anything else that will allow your customers to communicate with you.

Introvert

According to the Webster dictionary, an introvert is a person whose personality is characterized by introversion, a typically reserved or quiet person who tends to be introspective and enjoys being alone! So, in laymen terms you don't like being bothered. While I'm all for people staying out of my bubble and needing my own space, when it comes to your business you simply can't afford that luxury and still expect to grow. A great deal of balance is needed to be yourself and thrive. While you may not like dealing with strangers, introverts are typically big on relationships once established and that is exactly what you should leverage when showing up for your customers. Focusing on nurturing relationships with your brand. When dealing with your customers remove YOU from the conversation and focus on the WE. You don't have to be the face of your brand no matter what people say, and your customers don't know if you are a one woman show or team of 100's, so take it till you make it! Replace your 'I' with 'we' to remove the personalization and intimacy. For example, when customers have a question instead of "I would be happy to help" use "We would be happy to answer any questions" and if there is an issue replace "I" with "we", and "my" with "our." It will help you not take things personal and separate the business at hand.

People Pleasing

Okay, I don't mean to ruffle feathers, but we have to address this trait for baby servant leaders. People pleasing means you do things to please others regardless of how it makes you feel. A lot of times, people pleasing has some trauma attached and let me just say get help, so the shortcomings of others don't hold you back! Now, while you are searching for a therapist or going to those biweekly visits you will still need to figure out how to utilize this trait in a healthy way. For one, be very clear who you want to work with. I don't mean target audience. I mean fine tooth comb client profiling and persona creations. Knowing your who will help avoid requests that compromise your business goals.

Second, have professional boundaries. Know your non-negotiables and don't compromise them in efforts to please others. Third, focus on your can. Naturally, you dwell on your cant's, and you have trouble saying no, that's ok we just have to train the brain to focus on what opportunities saying no can create. Focus on what you can do to make others happy. No, you can't discount their products, but you can let them know when you have a sale coming or add them to your email list to know when there is a sale. No, you can't squeeze them in, but you can provide them some alternative professionals with more open scheduling. No, you can't take less but you can let them know what all they can get for what they have. It is all about the positive aspect.

Trusting

People trust you because you are honorable and worthy of their trust. This is such an awesome trait to carry when leveraged properly. Your ability to cultivate trust will allow you to sway any customer into a buyer naturally but be mindful of your boundaries. Be clear where you draw the relationship line with your customers and employees so they don't forget you are the CEO and you are not a pushover and you can and will be authoritative when needed.

There are plenty of other characteristics of a servant leader, but the core is empathy towards others, trust, humility, stewardship, and community. In my opinion, servant leadership is highly effective and very authentic. People can feel the genuineness of a servant leader. Even if you aren't a servant leader most naturally, you can adopt some strengths of servant leaders. No type of leader should be too busy or too high and mighty to serve. Great leaders are great because they are great servants. You just have to serve with a purpose. Serve your customers and employees because it serves and benefits your business. Make sure the two are always in alignment.

CHAPTER 4

THE OCD BUSINESS OWNER

"I <u>WILL</u> have order"

~*Delores Umbridge, Harry Potter*

I am a go with the flow kind of person. I schedule what I need to and wing it after that. I schedule kids' activities, appointments, meetings, and deadlines and let everything else just kind of fall into place. If the thought of living your life like that makes you cringe because you operate on a strict schedule, with a strict set of rules and an established set of responsibilities, this chapter my friend is for you. I swear I have come a long way adopting pieces of this leadership style even though it couldn't be any further from natural for me.

Just because you wrote it down or scheduled it doesn't make it right. According to the Mayo Clinic, "obsessive compulsive disorder features a pattern of thoughts and fears (obsessions) that lead you to do repetitive behaviors (compulsions)." Although you may not have actually been diagnosed with OCD, you may be someone that fears losing money, customers, failure, or something else so you do everything yourself, have a rule in place for everything, follow strict standardized processes, procedures and avoid networking or utilizing your support system. Although this type of person is not customer centric by nature, there is a leadership style with their name on it. This type of leader is most naturally a bureaucratic leader. Bureaucratic leader is indeed what it sounds like. It is restrictive, precise, and full of systems, rules, and processes. If you are this type of leader, I bet people don't particularly love working with you, do they? I also bet you'd rather do it yourself anyway. Like an executive coach once told me, "If you want to grow, you have to let go!" It is just that simple.

Have you ever worked for a company that was just all over the place and your first thought was, "Oh, hell no this is ridiculous?" This type of leader can be highly productive and efficient in an environment that lacks structure. Those companies that seem all over the place could benefit from a bureaucratic leadership style in executive leadership. Yes, executive leadership because when it comes to customers it is not one size fits all; although processes and systems are necessary for sustainable growth, empathy and flexibility are essential to building customer relationships. If I had to offer one piece of advice to a bureaucratic leader in terms of customer service and customer experience, it is to outsource in the beginning until you can afford your own team. When you can afford your own team start with leadership, a VP of customer service or customer experience, to director, to manager, to agents. Your VP will be your right hand in making sure policies are not only in place but changing and in alignment with the VOC or voice of customers. If you outsource your customer experience design but have to service your customer on your own in the beginning, it is important you leverage your personality in the right way.

Perfectionism

Perfectionism is always counterproductive, but especially in high level leadership. It is an unattainable goal, and it will stress you the hell out if that is what you aim for. Remove the word perfection from your vocab and replace it with greatness. Greatness means the quality of being great, distinguished, or eminent. Your desire for greatness can be an amazing thing if your energy is placed in the correct places. Instead of getting frustrated at customer questions and complaints or employee performance, focus on the details.

Focus on the why, not the what. Why are employees having trouble? Can training be improved? Why do customers have so many questions on social media, could you add policy and/or product information to your social media profile? Instead of getting annoyed at what all the customers are asking, focus on why they are asking and how you can improve your customer journey to eliminate those frequent questions. Instead of focusing on what customers are doing wrong, focus on what changes you can make. If your customers are reaching out on social media but you prefer your website or email, could you change your communication channels to be available where your ideal customers are? Customers are always changing, and customer experience design is continuous improvement. Focusing on improvements will shift your perfectionism mindset from how well things are going to how they can be better.

Favoritism

We can argue this but I rather not. Obsessive and perfectionist characteristics in leaders often yield environments of favoritism. In most studies you will find bureaucratic leadership is fair because the same rules and consequences apply to everyone and that is true to an extent. Although favoritism may not surface much in the workplace, when you are running a small business and wearing many hats, it can very much give off that impression to customers. Perception matters if you want to grow a successful business. It may not be conscious, but these unconscious biases will cause you to rely on and highlight those that are like you. It is important that you admit this type of behavior does exist because of your need to be perfect. It is hard to admit so take a moment right now, close the book if you need to. Now that we have admitted this characteristic, I want you to know that other type A personalities LOVE you because they feel all of your approval and acceptance. It is the customers that are different from you that you have to focus on. Focus on being fair. Focus on acknowledging the people that know but also the people that want to know.

Yes, they could have read that information at another touchpoint within your business, but they didn't so let it go and focus on the fact they want to know more about your business. Don't just respond to comments that make your business look good or ask questions you want others to know the answer to. Be consistent and fair. Be intentional. It is also important to give resources, meet customers where they are and answer questions but also give them the self-service resources available to them for when they have questions in the future.

Task Oriented

Let me tell you now, this right here is your SUPERPOWER! Anyone who tells you differently, is hating, big time! Sure, you can go overboard when you don't allow some room for the unexpected, at the end of the day all B.O.S.S. women need to be task oriented to some extent. Like my home girl Tina Fey said, "you can't be that kid at the top of the water slide, overthinking it. You have to go down the chute." While being task oriented can be highly effective in terms of productivity, if you get flustered when something comes up with a rushed deadline you can run into trouble. Depending on your business and industry, your ability to oversee sudden changes may be the key to the success or failure of your business. I, personally, don't think this is a trait you need to get rid of. I say organize it and give yourself a little bit of grace. Allow some room in your schedule for when shit happens, to avoid fluster and frustration. Dedicate time in both the morning and evening to your customers, in whatever capacity they need you; responding to emails or messages, calling people back, or any other type of communication your business offers. As a customer experience consultant, I highly recommend website chats but hold off on that communication channel until revenue picks up for you and you can afford to outsource or get internal help. I am not trying to overwhelm you by pushing the limits too far. BE realistic in your task and offer more channels at the right time. It will be helpful to create auto replies for written communication that acknowledges the communication and level sets when to expect a personalized response. I would encourage you to respond to all customer inquiries within 24 hours, any longer they may go to a competitor. If they go to a competitor, you have only yourself to blame, so save the comments like they aren't my target customer, or it wasn't meant to be. You fumbled your own bag with your entitlement and being lazy. When you dedicate your time to customer service, allow yourself enough time to respond, research and resolve. Be very detailed in your guidelines and standard operational procedures (SOP's), so when you are ready to pass the baton, you are setting your team up for your version of success.

Impersonal

When you place focus on performance, tasks and processes you often lose sight of people. Complete transparency, this common personality trait will not work when trying to build trust and relationships with your customers but it's all good making small changes can help you be perceived as more personable. Slow and steady wins the race. Here are a few tips to help you be more personable and build relationships with your customers.

1. Talk with a smile- It may be corny, but it is a scientific fact that smiling causes a chemical reaction within the body releasing hormones that reduce stress and encourage happiness such as dopamine and serotonin.

2. Use customer names whenever the opportunity allows- This is a simple action to make people feel acknowledged and respected.

3. Remember/ Track customer trends- remembering something about a customer's previous purchase, question, service, etc. will not only show you care but will allow you the opportunity to upsell your products in services.

4. Show empathy- Try and look at everything from the perspective of others before you deem yours as the one and only. Listen and acknowledge your understanding of others rather than whether you agree or not.

Bureaucratic leadership is not always looked at as the most effective type of leadership, but I am here to tell you that it has led to highly productive and efficient workplaces, just look at McDonald's, who prides themselves on being this type of organization. It's just when you are a one person show or have a people helping with your show, you have to modify what it looks like for the greater good of your business.

CHAPTER 5

THE HOME GIRL/BEST FRIEND BUSINESS OWNER

"A style does not go out of style as long as it adapts itself to its period. When there is an incompatibility between the style and a certain state of mind, it's never the style that triumphs."

~Coco Chanel

Most businesses like to call their customers family but are you someone that really treats your customer like extended family? Are you the kind of business owner that keeps it 100% all the time, super cool, and nickname your customers? You know the boo, babe, sis, chile, love and whatever other names people come up with it. Do you pride yourself on being relatable, trendy, and fun with your customers? This chapter is for you! Those of you that love people and people love you or you don't like people but are great at pretending so everyone wants to know you. You are what other entrepreneurs call the "popular" business owner. First off, embrace your ability to be liked, that in itself is something to be proud of and it does not come as easy for other business owners and leaders as it does for you. Your ability to adapt and your collaborative drive makes you a natural democratic leader.

Democratic leadership is a very inclusive and participative leadership style. It is actually really effective. This style of leadership encourages equality, participation, and a free flow of ideas. Collaborative leadership is great for morale building, innovation ideas and group productivity in the workplace but can be a total shit show in customer service, if you aren't careful. Don't get me wrong when strategically implemented, it can be great in the early part of your business to grow an audience, but it is not very sustainable for growth. This type of leadership will make it impossible to remove yourself from the day-to-day operations of your business without losing customer trust. If you plan to assign customer support at any point in your business, I suggest you make a few changes. I would encourage you to replace the 'I' with 'we' in your business, when interacting with customers and potential customers. The idea behind the "I" is to be relatable, but "we" is just as relatable because no one knows if you are a team of 1 or 100 but you, unless you are telling all your business, which, if you are definitely stop that. I encourage you to keep people you don't know off your personal social media, make two if it makes you feel better. My guess is, if you are this type of leader, it is too late for that but take a break from this book and clean it up or just make a new one whichever, is easier for you. Let people connect with your brand not actually you. You have to have boundaries for your customers to have them. Cleaning up your social media will allow for a much easier transition when you build your team.

Natural democratic leaders typically have the most difficult time of all leadership styles B.O.S.S.in up. Not because you aren't capable, but a lot of your success has been attributed to accessibility, inclusion and transparency and you are scared to let it go. I am here to confidently let you know you don't have to let it go, you just have to define it and put boundaries in place. You also need to be okay being a boss, not my acronym created for this book but simply a boss in its truest definition, a person in charge. Everyone is not equal, that is precisely why corporate hierarchies are in place. You are at the top of the food chain; it is important you remember that daily!

Discernment

You have the ability to judge well BUT keep it to yourself. Sometimes keeping it 100% means being real with yourself regarding appropriate times to share what you feel and when to keep it to yourself. I know what you are thinking, what does she expect me to do? I have an answer, use your gift like a B.O.S.S. Formulate a strategy for soliciting, hearing, and utilizing feedback. Take the time to review feedback from your customers and discern the valuable feedback from the useless feedback. Use your gift to grow your business, not lose customers. Judge feedback not people, which is not your job.

Service based business owners, prescreen your potential clients. Prepopulate a series of questions before accepting them as a client, to allow you the time to judge if they fit for your brand. Judge facts based on compatibility and credibility.

Inclusivity / Fairness

Engaging and making people feel included in your brand is your SUPERPOWER and why you are so loved. Have you ever heard the saying you can be lovable without being loved or likable without being liked? Those are words to live by! The same reason people love you is the same reason people don't take your small business seriously. The reason they contact you however they want, ask you for discounts, or cross all kinds of professional boundaries when communicating with you. To be a B.O.S.S. you have to show superintendence. Meaning you have to show you are the one in control of your business. You have to display your leadership position and ability. There should be zero confusion with customers or employees that you are in charge and running a business. It is important to have clear roles and responsibilities outlined in your business, you need to establish core values and service strategies, so the line of professionalism, transparency and relatability is never crossed.

You want customers to trust you enough to feel like they are making a quality purchase with an honorable brand, not enough to babysit their kids for the weekend, so keeping things professional and relatable won't hurt your business I promise. You should also have a clear list of what you will involve customer and employee input in and what you will not! The voice of your customers should help you reach a business goal if you are going to actually act on it. You need boundaries and implementing these things will function as your boundaries.

Anti-Bullying

You are thinking why this is even a thing, well because you like to include everyone so much you take it personal and to the extreme when someone doesn't play nice with others. You know like when you return money to customers because they are giving you a hard time. I am 100% for you maintaining your brand values through every interaction but I also want to hold you accountable for your position in your business, a B.O.S.S.

First off, we are not hanging up phones, ignoring emails, refunding money or any of that because a customer does not fit in your community and is throwing off the energy or whatever it is people say anymore. We are operating in leadership. The definition of leader is someone who leads. To lead is to guide or direct operations, activity, or performance. That means in order for you to operate in your position you have to be a bigger person. Don't back down or give up, we will simply provide an example of what we wish to see by how we conduct ourselves, without wavering. It won't always be easy but more often than not the tone will change because you controlled the situation and didn't let your customers, or the customer will decide they aren't a good fit for your brand. Don't get me wrong, there will be times when a refund will be the correct course of action, but it should never be because you lack self-control and awareness.

One of my least favorite quotes is that customers need to be better customers. A customer's only job is to make a purchase. It is not their job to influence behaviors, it is yours. Understand, everyone is not like you, nor does everyone expect a homegirl when doing business. There will be customers that hold you accountable in terms of being a B.O.S.S. and if you stay ready you don't have to get ready. When you are such a relatable business owner it is also easy for the anti-bully to become the bully on accident. Like Beyonce minds her business when people come for her, but the hive stays ready to go bat for her. I hate to tell you, you aren't Beyonce, it is a lot easier for an entertainer to remove themselves from the behaviors of their followers than it is for a micro small business owner.

Intelligence and Creativity

You love to include customers in your business because you are creative and innovative, and you love a challenge. You are also intelligent enough to bring new ideas to life. It is important to remember, everything doesn't have to be done immediately. You have plenty of time to plan and implement new ideas when your business needs something fresh. I would suggest a product innovation box for your business. It will give customers a place to share fun ideas they produce for you and you a point of reference when you are looking for something new that your customers want.

The theory that two is better than one is the democratic leadership approach. While it can be highly effective it is impossible to effectively manage without showing up for your business like a B.O.S.S. You didn't choose this leadership life, but it did choose you the moment you opened for business so put on your B.O.S.S. panties and own your spot at the top!

CHAPTER 6

THE FREE SPIRIT/ LAID BACK BUSINESS OWNER

"I like to be a free spirit. Some don't like that but that's just the way I am."

~*Princess Diana*

If controlling your energy and listening to the universe was a chapter, this would be it. The free spirit and laid-back business owner likes to work in their passion with little time or desire to work in other areas of their business. Don't get me wrong they still do but certainly not with the level of passion they do with their actual product or service. Now because of their natural attitude of zero damns given, this type of business owner has a great deal of comfort with mistakes, and I am sure you can imagine how that can be problematic. I would be lying if I told you I thought this was a healthy way to lead but it is indeed a method of leading and a place to start your leadership journey. There are two leadership styles this laid back, go with the flow kind of business owner can fall into, they are called Democratic and Laissez-Faire Leadership. They are the total opposite of the leadership style in chapter 2.

Democratic leaders love to include others in their decision-making process and delegate often. Although Democratic Leaders delegate they still lead the decision-making process. Unlike Laissez Faire leaders, which also delegates but are more hands off. Laissez Faire leadership style is not the most productive, while you learn yourself as a leader and learn how to adapt different styles, you can still operate like a B.O.S.S. with this as your primary Leadership style.

Laissez-Faire leadership encourages personal growth and innovation. Even with those pros I'm not sure they outweigh the cons because there is lack of clarity in roles and responsibilities as well as low accountability. I'm not trying to change you, I promise, I'm just making you aware of the great challenges you may face by owning this laid-back hands-off leadership style. Let's take a look at your strengths and how you can use them to B.O.S.S. up.

Creative

Free spirit and laid back is the culture of creativity, so it is no shock creativity thrives under laissez-faire leadership. This is a double-edged strength internally building a culture in which creativity and thinking outside the box is encouraged can be extremely good in terms of innovations, but when it comes to the early stages of your business this often carries over to your consumers. That will become an overwhelming, non-sustainable shit show. You have to have boundaries.

It is crucial that you have structure in your business. You need hours of operation and detailed order/ booking forms. I know that last part is going to be hard because you want to be able to just do you and if you do you, your customers are free to do them and ain't nobody got time for that. Not because we don't want to make customers happy because I'm all about customer centricity, but I also want your business to thrive and in order to align the two, we have to know what happiness looks like for customers that are within your abilities and most importantly their price point. If you're in a product-based business, try and send product samples and examples prior to production. If you are in a service-based business before services are rendered create a clear summary of services, so expectations are very clear and objective!

Laid Back

The time will come when you can delegate more in your business and can remove yourself from some of the day-to-day tasks should you choose but be honest with yourself regarding if it is truly feasible for your business or just convenient for you. Going with the flow will be all good when you are able to build a dream team. Yes, I mean dream team! If being relaxed is a goal of yours, you will be putting a lot of trust in others, so you will need the best and most qualified individuals to make that happen. Some people can get away with hiring friends and family in their business. I don't think that would be a good idea for you as this type of leader. It will be beneficial for you to do things yourself and outsource until you can afford the absolute best! I understand creativity thrives in a relaxed environment but a bunch of innovative ideas from a bunch of inexperienced people will cost you eventually and although delegation will probably become your super power it can cost you tons of time and money if done before you are ready.

Laid back, is not the way to be when it comes to customers. You can be flexible; you can be relatable but not laid back. You have to ablt to take control when needed. The definition of laid back is to be relaxed and easy going, absolutely nothing about being a business owner is relaxed and easy going, so that is a good indication something isn't right. Just like any other relationship, being too laid back will get you run over and run down, and no one has time for that. Your carefree personality comes off authentic so use it to build trust and relationships with your customers but when it is time to make the sale, it is important you have clear and concise instructions and policies in place. Take my word for it, if you haven't already learned the hard way, if you are too relaxed with your customers, they will not respect you or your business. When customers don't respect your business, they think they have the ability to make special requests, not follow policies and make demands. There is a difference between someone liking you and respecting you. To like someone means to find them enjoyable and satisfactory. To respect someone means to consider them worthy of high regard. So, unless you plan to go for drinks with your customers you want to be respected while also being likable, not to be liked.

Trusting

You have a unique ability to assume innocence and see the best in people. I envy it because my guard stays up. Most free spirit business owners believe things happen for a reason and things people are aligned how they should be. I believe that to be true as well, but I also believe we choose who we allow in our space and there should be a vetting process before we just go with the flow. In business your trust should be extended via empathy, relationship building and policy creation. Trust is a two-way street, so it is unfair to approach your business being overly trusting. You gain others' trust by displaying your expertise, giving honest feedback, and acknowledging feedback with a result driven approach and consistency. Your customers will gain trust with loyalty and referrals. Your employees gain trust with consistency, accountability, performance, and whatever other metrics you decide. The point is you have to make people work to be in your trust circle.

Personal Awareness

Free spirit people are super in tune with their emotions and are very protective of maintaining their energy and mood. I think this is impressive! Personal Awareness is just a component of what it takes to have a high EQ. You need to not only know yourself and your triggers but know how to self-regulate. As a B.O.S.S. you can't always avoid people in situations that shift your mood, so you have to learn to control it. So, no more refunded money back because your energy is off and all that. Instead, we are going to self-regulate when put in challenging situations. A key to self-regulation is establishing core values and knowing your calming mechanisms, for some it is meditation. If you are like me and haven't quite mastered that, practice deep breathing and writing down your first thoughts and negative thoughts and throw them away. It's better than saying it aloud.

Laissez Faire leadership style is very difficult to maintain so it is extremely important to educate yourself on other leadership styles and adapt as needed. I don't want you to change who you are I just want you to be flexible and maintain your B.O.S.S. status in EVERY situation.

CHAPTER 7

THE FREEBIE BUSINESS OWNER

"Reward behavior you want repeated."

~Unknown

You ever see a small business that stay giving bomb discounts or always running a giveaway? Or are you this person? I have never met a business owner like this who does it without logic. We are all told as business owners these things grow your audience and they increase your sales but never talk about if it is sustainable or what kind of customers are attracted to "free." Have you ever heard the saying, "Nothing worth having is free"? I don't know if I agree with that in its entirety, but I do believe free and discounted should be sparingly and provided when earned....... Freebie business owners typically see the grand picture when giving stuff away, they just lack strategy. Reality is if you can get your product in the hands of more people and provide an experience that builds relationships you will foster loyal customers.

I am sure you are not giving products and services away because you don't want to be successful or your calling in life is just to give endlessly with no evidence of ever reaping the benefits of what you have sown. You do it because you have a great product or service, and you just want people to know about it, so you have potential customers do stuff for you that benefit you in exchange for your product or service. This is common. This type of leader is a transactional leader. Transactional leaders view relationships as an exchange and believe in rewarding good behavior and punishing bad behavior. Unbelievably, most established transactional leaders are men. I don't think it is necessarily because women aren't this type of leader, I think we are either afraid of society labels of this type of woman or don't know how to effectively lead in this way. Either way, own your shit! Gender is not a specification for any type of leadership! You are not an opportunist. You are not a gold digger. You are not a user. You are brilliant and you understand the power in cause-and-effect relationships. You just need to B.O.S.S. up.

Transactional

Let's start with the obvious you move with purpose; you give with the expectation to receive. There is nothing wrong with that, just make sure you are intentional. Free always brings a certain type of customer, not your ideal customer so it is a great possibility free won't result in a long-term relationship. I do think promotions are good when growing your audience, so it is important to be strategic with your promotions. Instead of following me for something free or chance to win something free, you can request a desired action in exchange for a chance to win a gift card or to be provided a discount code. This will still allow you to get some money if you properly calculate the credit. But make sure you are not just doing promotions that are benefiting you in barely anyway. A Follow does not mean a sale they can unfollow you, just like them following you doesn't guarantee them a chance to win. Believe it or not some people may get bitter if they don't win. You also want to pre plan sales with the end goal in mind. How much do you want to make? How much can you discount and still make your profit goal? You do not have to sacrifice business needs for customers' needs they should always align when you are customer centric. You want to spend most of this strength on creating a strategic loyalty/ reward program to keep customers coming back and telling people about your brand. Transactions only work so much when building relationships, it is important you don't get complacent. Focus on developing your empathy. Emotional loyalty is always more loyal than behavioral.

Goal Driven

Transactional leaders are focused on the results and goals. It is imperative you establish clear business goals and key performance indicators or KPIs. You need to know exactly what you need to accomplish as well as what your customers want. Make sure you do some market research to identify the want so you aren't doing what sounds good to you but no one else and figure out what you wish to accomplish with each transaction. KPIs measure your performance towards your business goals, that way you can PIVOT when your freebies are not giving what they should be. (For more information on establishing KPIs visit www.bitchorboss.org)

Simple and to the point

You are great at articulating your rewards and set my standards and expectations. Simplicity is your friend because it leaves little room for disappointment, confusion, or anything extra. That is not a bad thing all the time but that often sends you to giveaways to get your desire or outcome, don't get more simply than that. Instead, I challenge you to ask your target audience what type of promotions they enjoy and simplify that type of promotion and explain the desired outcome, so it is clear and to the point. Another thing to remember is, it's okay to be direct and to the point as long as you explain. Say what you have to say and explain why you said it to show you care.

Practical

Practicality to an extent is essential for growing a sustainable business, however, you are very pragmatic in your approach. You are overly consumed with considering risk and obstacles. You don't want to talk yourself out of opportunities, growth, and improvements. Overly practical people usually suffer from risk aversion. Investments are all about taking risk and risk management. Both risk taking and risk aversion are necessary but don't be so consumed with one you avoid the other. Investments in customer service and customer experience often take time to see the ROI but you have to be willing to see the big picture and the long-term goal. Don't let your practicality cause you to be complacent and your business to be stagnant.

Transactional leadership definitely is effective when working to achieve goals just make sure your goals are clearly defined. This systematic approach to leading is pretty fair and easy to understand. Be careful of being so structured you miss opportunities to be innovative in your field.

CHAPTER 8

THE MAMA BEAR BUSINESS OWNER

"What doesn't kill you makes you stronger. Stand a little taller."

~Kelly Clarkson

If parenting was a leadership style this is it. One thing about a mother, more often than not they see the very best in their kids. Sure, they identify opportunities for growth, but they wholeheartedly believe if they put their minds to it, they can do anything, disregarding genetics, and any other obvious obstacle. This is me. I'm naturally this type of leader, one that encourages, one that develops, one that focuses on authentic and one that tries to assume innocence. As a mom of four and the oldest girl of my siblings, it's legit built in me. I lead by example. I am always looking to new ways of doing things and learn. These types of business owners typically have very high EQ's. What I am describing is a transformational leader. Although, one of the most hands on and time-consuming leadership styles, transformational leadership is also one of the most effective leadership styles when practiced properly, if for no reason other than Oprah Winfrey is a transformation leader.

Transformational leaders are able to identify the strengths and weaknesses in others effortlessly. They are supportive and teach rather than command. This style is centered on inspiring and motivating. They motivate using enthusiasm and empowerment. Internally that can obviously encourage great performance from motivated employees and with customers it can teach them how to treat your brand. Customers can have a lot of personalities, so it takes discipline of course but just like your kids have different personalities you just have to teach them a little different. Just like any other leadership style you may have to combine this leadership style with transactional leadership when dealing with employees to get results, depending on the person. Your personality will let you transform about any customer or situation when used strategically.

H.B.I.C./ Leadership

You are a natural born leader indeed, because well we have to be, but consumers are grown adults and you can't treat them like your kids or husband. Because you said so isn't going to cut it. You have to have policies and values that guide customers in dealing with your brand and you have to show them, so it becomes a habit. Remember to be respectful. There is a difference between being a B.O.S.S.

and being bossy, when working with adults you want to avoid the ladder. Your comfort you have in being in charge is great, you understand the hard part of the assignment, the easy part is practicing what you preach. The toxic mindset a lot of us grew up with, "do what I say not what I do" isn't really practice and it is the total opposite of B.O.S.S. behavior.

Developmental/ Transformational

Nurturing comes naturally and what you nurture will grow. You have the ability to make others be their best, the key is how you do it. You can't just tell people what they are going to do and not going to do, instead you slow them down by what you do and having clear policies. Just like your kids will try you as will customers and once they see they are not getting the reaction they thought, they will conform to appropriate behavior. For example, if you have policies regarding communication channels but some customers don't follow them instead of ignoring them redirect that behavior to encourage a different behavior. Create a template reply advising this is not the correct channel of communication and advise what is.

Inspirational

You may not consider yourself a role model, and it may drive you crazy others do but it is a part of who you are. It's not because you are perfect. It is because people trust you, respect you and find it natural to want to mimic your behaviors. It is important you look the part. Your ability to tap into your natural B.O.S.S.-ness is going to determine exactly how difficult your customers will be. I know it is not fair and you are human but if this is your primary leadership style it comes with the territory most naturally. You don't match energy, you control it.

Giving

A giving heart is a good heart but can cause you to never make any money. You have to take care of the aspects and people generating your revenue before you start giving stuff away for free. Don't give to others before giving to yourself. You can't cater to everyone and there is no point in trying. It is okay to have a target customer persona and it's okay if everyone doesn't fit. Be okay knowing some people can't afford you, don't discount it to accommodate. Be okay knowing some people have a crappy work ethic, be okay passing on collaborating with them. Don't get caught up on who you can't help, focus on who you have and can. Nurture those relationships and figure out how you can continue to add value.

Transform means to change in character or condition, if you have not tapped into your individual B.O.S.S. and already have a brand that could use some major changes I recommend adopting this leadership style, even if it's not your most primary. The superpower for this leadership style is the ability to transform and develop the skills and qualities of others.

CHAPTER 9

UNLEARN TO RELEARN

"The first problem for all of us, men, and woman, is not to learn but to unlearn. We are filled with the popular wisdom of several centuries just past, and we are terrified to give it up. Patriotism means obedience, age means wisdom, woman means submission, black means inferior: these are preconceptions imbedded so deeply in our thinking that we honestly may not know that they are there."

~ Gloria Steinem

In the business world, we tend to be limited by our academic backgrounds. But since our education is fragmented, we cannot fully benefit from it. Like turning the pages of a book, it's important to move on to new information once you've mastered the previous topic. Being a B.O.S.S. requires elevation, in every aspect. You have to elevate yourself beyond an employee mindset, beyond some of the things you grew up learning, beyond your fear of speaking up because you are afraid of how you will be perceived, beyond dumbing yourself down to make other people feel better, beyond thinking presentation doesn't matter and beyond making choices that go against your core values to please others.

To elevate means to raise to a more important or impressive level. Plenty of business owners have reached a certain version of success so they start acting as though they have really elevated, when in reality they have not at all; hence the B.O.S.S. Imposter trying to cover herself. They are still presenting themselves to the world with a low-level mindset. Money doesn't make you a B.O.S.S., elevation and leadership does. To be a B.O.S.S. the old way of doing things isn't going to cut it. You have to get control of your emotions and hold yourself accountable. You have to not only follow rules but implement them. Doing the bare minimum will get you the bare minimum. Modern society is constantly evolving and B.O.S.S.es have to evolve with it.

To make matters worse, our thoughts are notoriously resistant to change, thus the imposition of reality has profound effects on us. A person might practice unlearning by expanding their awareness and critically examining their own thought processes and behavior. Unlearning is not forgetting, but rather shaping one's mental habits in order to leave the world as it is and build a new one. In fact, many organizations provide formal leadership training for their personnel. Typical subjects covered in such classes include effective communication, resolving conflicts, working together as a team, etc.

If you want to be a B.O.S.S., you have to keep trying with grace and fortitude. To get it right, we must also abandon our established practices in favor of exploring novel approaches. Making our brains realize why we shouldn't employ the previous way makes the task even more challenging. The process of learning, unlearning, and retraining brings a childlike purity that is vital to the natural growth of any organization. To unlearn, one must first realize that one's current approach is ineffective.

In order to advance an enterprise, it is vital to engage in the practice of unlearning. To make something truly original, we must discard our conventional ways of thinking and doing. Curiosity is the driving force for creative breakthroughs, such as the completion of a new project or the sealing of a deal with an unexpected client. With unlearning, you may do things at your own pace and remove roadblocks to your development.

Be Heard & Command Respect

Since the beginning of time women have been silencing their voice out of fear of what others may think or to make others comfortable. In order for you to be a B.O.S.S. you have to not only acknowledge but embrace and celebrate your voice. Speaking up does not make you a B.I.T.C.H., it makes you a woman doing her job, when you are in fact in a position of leadership. Speaking up doesn't make you mannerless as long as you are equally as willing to hear others and not being rude. It is truly not what you say, it is how you say it. Speaking up is the only way to get stuff done! You have not because you ask not. Be professional and kind while also being firm because you have a business to run. Having a voice does not mean you are operating in masculinity it means you are operating in leadership. You can be feminine and have an opinion and command respect. You don't have to choose. Don't straddle the fence to make others comfortable, it diminishes credibility in your voice, pick a side unapologetically and stand on it. One of the greatest powers of femininity is its power of influence over others.

To earn respect, you must confront others squarely in the face. If you want to know why, just ask and listen. It's not necessary for you to always be the one to initiate conflict; doing so labels you as a B.I.T.C.H. Still, it's your responsibility to push back against their presumptions. If you're in business, I can assure you that "why are we doing this?" is the question no one likes to hear. It demonstrates your awareness and ability to put others on the defensive. Particularly in the early stages, you should expect to be ignored, mocked, pestered, and generally avoided. One of my rivals is you. The fastest way to get respect and establish yourself as a strong opponent is to directly contradict their preconceived notions of you.

You should never whine, defend, or apologise. Grumblers are looked down upon, while those who try to explain things are never taken seriously. If you're going to do something, do it because you WANT to, not because you feel like you have to. Execution gives the impression that you are in charge and a leader. Never say sorry for making an effort to accomplish what you believe to be right or what is required. Respect may only be gained by an apology if the offender admits to having done wrong. The failure of a strategy, however, is not grounds for apologies. You may simply state that just because your idea was unsuccessful does not imply that any of the alternatives would have been any more fruitful.

To add, if you desire genuine and widespread respect, you should skip learning the tactics of the profession and instead learn the skill itself. Respect is earned only through proven skill and achievement. This might be a time-consuming process at first, especially for novices. You gain that time by inquiring about something. Try your best at work and never, ever be spotted holding a coffee mug. Dress more formally than the other sex. If you can convince them that you belong in a leadership role, you will be promoted. If you portray yourself as troublesome, that is exactly what you will become. If you dress like a bum, people will want to pick you up. Put on an air of authority and people will treat you with more deference. Appearances are what they are. Perception is the foundation of reality. In addition, remember that saying or doing nothing is almost always the best option. One should never waste an opportunity to be quiet. Also, be careful to never, ever embellish your statements. Constantly be prepared with a workable answer to every issue, and understate your difficulties. In fact, that's the main reason for your employment. You're either a person who can help others solve problems or a problem that prevents others from doing so. Avoid the necessity for a solution. Ever. Keep an optimistic, can-do mindset at all times. This does NOT imply being a cheesy people-pleaser; rather, it calls for an unwavering belief that one can learn from any experience, no matter how negative it may seem at the time.

Maintain a positive relationship with your superiors by consistently reaching out to them for guidance. Treat yourself with dignity and tell the world about it. If you walk around exuding assurance in yourself and a can-do attitude while keeping your cool, you'll be able to intimidate the hell out of everybody you come across. If everything else fails, try challenging their beliefs publicly while maintaining a cheerful appearance. They'll run for cover again.

Woman≠Superhuman

In the workforce, women have to work twice as hard to just be seen, let alone be equal and appreciated. It sucks so don't you dare take that energy into your business. There is no prize for overwhelming yourself, just exhaustion, extra weight, hair loss and some other side effects no one wants. Smart work is the key, not hard work. Think about how many times you worked for someone in leadership that had you doing their work. Whether or not they gave you credit is not the point, the point is good leaders know how to delegate to those capable of getting things done. I know people mean well when they say things like, "you can do it" and "you are so strong," but it sets us up to work harder than we need to in the name of being strong. Strong is overrated. The strong survive the smart thrive.

We need to be able to say we need help and actually get the help when your funds allow. Think about it, when you force yourself to do things beyond your capacity, how much of it truly gets 100%. Half assing is not B.O.S.S. behavior so when you begin to feel stretched too far get some help because something is not always better than nothing when it can be done right. Superheroes are fictional, and a title we can never really live up to, but heroes exist in our everyday lives. A hero is a person who is admired for their courage, outstanding achievements, or noble qualities.

A B.O.S.S. is a hero, in its true form not in an imaginary world. Know your strengths and weaknesses and while you always want to improve your weaknesses, be courageous in delegating accordingly. That is just one of many things you need to unlearn to elevate.

The power is in your yes

Ever think about how much of an impact a simple "yes" from a business can have on a customer' What I've found is that this seemingly innocuous confirmation — that we can do what the other person wants us to do — has the ability to lay the groundwork for deep and lasting bonds between two people.

Being a woman, I know how difficult it is to learn to say no. We are socialized to be nurturers and nurtureees. Despite the importance of developing the ability to decline service requests, the strength of a customer service professional is in their ability to enthusiastically accept them. Service to consumers is a process that entails assisting them at every stage of their interaction with a company. When you say no, the journey comes to a halt, but when you say yes, you may change the course of their travels.

Though it's tempting to simply say "no" in answer to a customer's request, it's important to see the opportunity that "no" presents. Therein lies the secret of success. Not at this time, but clients who sign up for your email list will be the first to know about any future discounts or freebies. You don't take returns, but would you consider offering a discount on future purchases as a way to retain customers? Although you do not offer replacements for missing mail, could you contact the post office and file a report on the customer's behalf? You can contradict yourself by simultaneously denying and accepting something.

Others will be attracted to you if you are a "yes" person because they will think you are a cheerful, optimistic person. Your mental health and the mental health of others around you will suffer if you have a habit of continually finding fault or always saying "no." If you want to expand your business, you need to convince people that you can accomplish something that no one has ever accomplished before. You have access to the means and the expertise necessary; unfortunately, you have not yet been given the chance to demonstrate your worth. A potential investor may be the one who asks. It could make you feel like a deer caught in headlights. Say "yes" despite the glare of the spotlights if you know what you're doing and have all you need to get the job done.

Even if it seems like a waste of time and money at first, saying yes can be beneficial to your company's growth in many ways. It will help you develop into a more upbeat and enjoyable companion. Since you made such a good first impression, you may expect to be the first vendor the buyer contacts. If an investor is looking to back a company, yours will be the one they choose because they can tell that you have the self-assurance of someone who is serious about making progress and expanding their firm.

It Does Matter What You Make People Think

There is a widespread sense of guilt among women for caring so much about what men think of them. This has led them to the conclusion that they are a weak person. However, it's important to consider the opinions of others for more than vanity's sake.

To begin with, this assertion is true in two ways, first a B.O.S.S. must be receptive to feedback. Feedback creates opportunities to be better. Second, people buy into people and things they trust and like and sometimes that is visual. People don't know the inside of you until they have already encountered the exterior. Everyone is taught it doesn't matter what people think about you as long as you are happy with yourself. I really want to know the logic behind that because it really isn't completely true. If those days ever existed, they certainly don't anymore. While you should operate in your purpose and not expect or care if anyone else understands or thinks, what people think about you is a direct reflection of your brand in the beginning. It is inevitable.

Social media is public information, based on external the image you are giving off matters. You can't call yourself a brand manager and can't manage to control your own tongue. You can't expect people to take your image seriously if you don't. You have to do the inner work to be a B.O.S.S. and it is hard.... mind, body, and soul. I am not saying you change who you are for others that would be insane, but you have to do the work. The *SHOWING* is real in the acronym and it is not by mistake. You have to not just be mentally at your best but also physically. I don't mean you need to be skinny or in designer clothes, but you do need to be put together. The way you present yourself to your customers or potential customers needs to be whole. Your version of whole will not look like someone else's version of whole, but you have to do the work to figure out what that looks like to you.

People are visual, and while often subconscious, a lot of judgements of you are preconceived by others before you even get to show your value any other way, so it is important to look your best. Don't consume yourself with what others think but definitely think about how you wish to present yourself and your brand to the world.

People are social creatures, therefore it's fair to argue that picking up on the reactions of others around you might

70

provide you insight into the health of your connections. You are aware of whether or if your actions have alienated or won over others. When you care about those relationships, you care about what those people think. While you might be prepared to risk hurting a loved one's feelings in order to solve a problem, you ultimately want to make amends or move past the issue. Listening to and responding to people's opinions can help you succeed in life and preserve important connections. Everyone, even the most self-reliant, is profoundly influenced by the opinions of those around them.

The trouble with worrying about what other people think arises when you let that worry cloud your judgment or, even worse, when you stop thinking for yourself in an effort to please others. The ability to trust one's own judgment in any given circumstance is crucial. If you don't, then you should start actively thinking about your past, present, and future experiences, as well as your wants, needs, and desires.

The Customer Is Always Right

The more satisfied consumers we have, the more money we can make from each sale. It's a cliche, but the saying, "the customer is always right," is a cornerstone of many successful business philosophies. It's a sign that businesses recognize their customers as priceless resources essential to their success. This phenomenon has been around for ages and has been both criticized and praised by many. Some people think it's unfair because it benefits people who don't deserve it while making others unhappy. On the other hand, those who support it argue that it is significant because it stands for good business practices and a promise to deliver superior goods and services.

When you work for someone, it sounds like bull shit but when you work for yourself you need to understand the phrase. Customers are the reason you are in business and although the way they manage requests or the request itself is not always the best without them there would be no business. Customers are not business owners they didn't sign up for leadership so they may not have signed up to do the internal work it requires to be a B.O.S.S. and that is ok.

Instead of worrying about the ridiculous request of customers or the nasty tone, listen to the underlying context of what is being said. Customers always have a right to feel how they feel. As a B.O.S.S. It is up to you to determine why they feel that way and figure out what you can do to prevent it in the future.

Many businesses continue to adhere to the adage "the customer is always right" because they recognize the critical role customers play in the continuation and growth of their operations. Without buyers, a business is just a bunch of individuals putting in effort to create something that nobody wants. The issue has been around for a while because it is every company's primary objective to provide its customers with the best possible goods and services. As a result, putting the needs of the customer first should be the primary goal of any enterprise. Customer unhappiness has been a major factor in the demise of numerous companies. In such instances, failure resulted from a drop in sales and an exodus of customers. A company's reputation might take a hit if its customers express dissatisfaction in written form. Rebuilding a company's reputation after it has been damaged is no easy task. Some businesses, for instance, invest billions in CSR initiatives to recover from public relations disasters that drive away customers.

One form of B.O.S.S.-approved business conduct is placing the needs of consumers ahead of all else. Reputation and credibility are bolstered when a company listens carefully to its customers, provides excellent service, welcomes their comments, and keeps them informed. A customer deserves kindness and consideration. When customers are treated well, businesses see increased loyalty, brand recognition, and revenue as a result.

Customers who leave a firm satisfied are invaluable, as they will likely return or recommend it to others. Growing one's clientele is an objective shared by all commercial enterprises. The key to expansion and success in today's technologically savvy world is maintaining happy consumers, as there are many venues for customers to voice their opinions about businesses. To help them decide what to buy, many consumers now first check online reviews of the goods. If a company consistently receives high marks from its customers, it's likely because it provides superior service and products.

When you operate under the premise that the client is always right, you force yourself to provide exceptional service to them. It has been proven via studies that the quality of a customer's experience is the key factor in determining whether or not that consumer will remain loyal to a firm or look elsewhere.

The unhappiness of current customers is used as a marketing tool by competitors. Therefore, it's more cost-effective in the long run to invest in customers' happiness rather than risk having them defect to the competition. As an example, you may incorporate after-sale services like discounts and loyalty programs to keep customers coming back. There are numerous approaches one can take to obtain the highest levels of customer satisfaction. Some examples include being quick to reply, getting to know customers on a personal level through encounters, admitting and rectifying errors, demonstrating empathy for customers, and planning for the future.

Customers are essential to the success of every organization because they drive revenue, expand customer bases, and promote brands for free. People are more likely to recommend a company to their friends if they have a positive experience with that company. In addition, they contribute to a company's brand and reputation positively through their online reviews. Dissatisfied customers look elsewhere, so it's in everyone's best interest for businesses to focus on keeping them happy.

Treat people how they want to be treated

It is not about you. I know we are taught from the time we are young to treat others the way you want to be treated but it is not really applicable at this level of leadership. If you treat me the way you expect to be treated, there is a good chance you will disgust me. Possibly not at first, but eventually, yes. Why? For the simple reason that I am not you; therefore, my thoughts and values are not yours (they may be close, but they are not identical), and neither is my style of communication. Consequently, treating me as you would like to be treated implies that we are same, which is obviously not the case. It's easy to assume that we're all the same, yet even seemingly minor preferences like whether or not you take milk in your tea or coffee reveal our unique personalities. There is a lot of variety among us. So many factors—the family you were raised in, the friends you kept, the teachers who made an impression on you, the experiences you had and the meaning you gave them—contributed to making each of us who we are today. We all see the world in slightly different ways, which is why the adage "treat others as you would like to be treated" might not be very helpful right now.

There will be some people who are swayed by your strategy, but there will also be some who are completely against it. And it's not so much that they don't agree with your ideas as they do with the way you've presented them, by treating them as you would like to be treated.

Becoming a Powerful B.O.S.S. Begins With Treating Others How They Would Like To Be Treated

Not all employees will thrive under the same type of leadership you do and that doesn't make them a bad employee, it means you need to adapt. Most successful businesses are customer centric. It is the way of the world now. In order to be customer centric you have to know your customers and act based on who they are. I mean everyone can't be a B.O.S.S. like you and you can't treat them as such. Treating people the way you want to be treated may work if you are your ideal customer but oftentimes that is not the case, and you have to treat people how they want to be treated in order to build trust and loyal relationships.

Boundaries ≠ Convenience

I am not sure if we were taught this or if it is our human entitlement, but boundaries don't mean convenience. The first thing a B.I.T.C.H. does is use boundaries as an excuse for pure nonsense. Establishing boundaries means you have set rules and policies in place in your business, and you stick to them. When leading a successful business, rules and policies are made with the customer in mind so boundaries are fair and easy but if you made them based on your school schedule, kids sport practice, or just whatever makes you feel good you should not be surprised your customers don't respect your rules and policies.

You can't be open from 10am-2pm because your kid has soccer practice and your target audience is working moms, they are at work and following your rules is not realistic for them. You can't have 80% baby boomer clientele and wonder why they are not sending you orders online like you want but calling you and sending an email. They barely use computers let alone get on websites, read the room. You can't have generation z as target customers and mad they are sending you DM's; social media is their generation. You have to learn your audience when creating boundaries and stick to them. It is not about you. Eventually in your business you will be able to work when it is convenient for you but in the beginning, you really need to establish boundaries based on your customer base and their needs.

There will always be something you have to unlearn to unlock different levels of success and leadership and be ok doing it. Embrace the journey. You aren't a rebel; you elevate and focus on the big picture. Success will require constant cycles of unlearning, learning, relearning, and evolving. It is not about letting go of what you know and have been taught, it is about having the courage to question it and its truth in your life. Always be open to new ideas and ways of thinking, admit when things you were taught don't work for you and don't be afraid to amend what you once knew.

CHAPTER10

TO BECOME A GOOD BOSS, YOU SHOULD BE THE BEST VERSION OF YOU FOR YOUR CUSTOMERS EACH AND EVERY DAY

In order to become the finest version of yourself, you must eliminate your self-limiting beliefs. Realizing one's full potential does not necessitate a problem-free existence. True self-actualization is possible despite continuing challenges.

Innumerable media outlets, including movies, novels, and even our own parents, have contributed to perpetuating this falsehood. We've been instructed to keep our noses to the grindstone. And then, finally, after all those years of hard work, the miracles begin to occur. We can't be proud of ourselves until we put in a lot of effort. But the reality is that modern life is extremely hectic. All of us are always looking for something better, and we never seem satisfied with what we have. However, there has been a shift in recent years toward inside rather than outward pursuit of happiness. The things we've done are more important to us than the things we've bought. In lieu of monetary stability, we prioritize mobility. Additionally, our primary goal is to develop into our true selves. To be the best version of oneself, what does that even entail?, What exactly do we mean when we say "realize your potential"?

In your pursuit of self-knowledge, self-assurance, and happiness, these are among the questions you have probably asked yourself. When you don't feel like you're making progress toward your goals, it's time to start asking the big questions that will help you learn how to develop yourself to your fullest potential.

True self-discovery is arduous. In other words, bravery and perseverance are required. To become closer to your true self, you have to abandon the deceiving ideas you've been feeding yourself. The secret to success is to show what really motivates you, not just the superficial factors like money or power. Your final goal in life. If you're worried about making changes to better yourself, keep in mind: Each and every one of us has our own special set of qualities. Given that you have unique goals, interests, and abilities, you can't compare your life to someone else's and expect to achieve the same level of success. Since everyone's journey is unique, there is no definitive plan or perfect conclusion.

Your standards and values are the bedrock of your decision-making and the path to being the best version of yourself. What you're willing to accept in life is defined by your standards, while your values determine who you are.

How willing are you to settle for anything less than your full, magnificent, and potent potential?

Discovering your core beliefs, interests, and passions is the first step in becoming the most authentic version of yourself. Practice talking to yourself like you would on a first date. Pretend your ideal self is sitting next to you and ask, "What do you like to do in your spare time?" Which of these people do you find yourself most comfortable with? How would you like to change the world? If you could relive one moment in your life, what would it be? Put your whole heart into your responses.

Pay attention to how you feel as the talk progresses. It's likely that if you're feeling "bad" emotions like anxiety or rage, you're actually communicating with yourself in a subliminal way that's clouded by those feelings. Investigate the source of the emotion more thoroughly. Do you worry that you won't be able to find yourself? Are you terrified of what you'll find when you dive deep? Although it's human nature to question whether or not we measure up, the reality is that we're perfect as we are. Getting in touch with this core you is what will allow you to flourish. You can begin working toward your ideal self once you've settled on who it is you aspire to be. Plan your journey to your best self by beginning with the destination in mind. Pursuing one's own sense of fulfillment is a worthy objective. You're on the correct path if you want to make a difference in the world while being true to who you are.

Habits That Will Help You Become the Best Version of Yourself

DISCARD SELF-LIMITING IDEAS: You are already who you think you are, but are you also who you could be? The majority of people are unable to achieve their full potential because of restricting beliefs. Identifying and discarding the self-defeating ideas that have been holding you back is the first step in becoming your true, authentic self.

Rather than treating them as optional, make the following your absolute musts: It's impossible to be your best self if you harbor any resentment about your past actions. If you want to succeed, you have to push yourself outside of your comfort zone, take chances, and fail (yes, fail). It's time to stop telling yourself you "should" do something and really do it. Tony suggests using the rocking chair test. Picture yourself as a wise old man or woman contemplating your life from the comfort of your gray hair. Which of your accomplishments do you hold closest to your heart? In what ways do you feel regret? Find out what you absolutely need to have by doing this.

Tolerance of Current Practice: One of the keys to reaching your full potential is developing the ability to accept life exactly as it is presented to you. Rather than longing for a different outcome, you make the best of the circumstances at hand, such as a wet day when you had planned an outside event. Additionally, it may mean that you learn to embrace the unknowns in your life. Or it could

81

indicate that you try to be less idealistic and more open to alternative explanations.

Focusing on what you do well will make you even better at it, and you'll grow into a more complete person as a result. Keeping your attention on your advantages is equally crucial when you encounter difficulties. Boosting your strengths helps you remember your unique contributions and overcome any challenges you face.

Adopt a growth mindset because no one has only strengths. To become the best version of ourselves, we must all address our weaknesses. And they do so by adopting a development mindset, the secret weapon of those who consistently succeed. In their minds, there are no such things as weaknesses. Nothing but room for development is ahead. They don't dwell on their shortcomings but rather on the ways in which they might better themselves and work toward that end.

Many people say, "Live authentically," but what does it even mean? To live an authentic life, you must be true to yourself and refrain from deceiving others or neglecting your own wants and needs. For some people, this could entail caring less about what others think. You disregard the advice of others and instead act on the advice of your heart, as well as the desires of your clients, rather than on the basis of what others think you should do. To succeed in business, you need to do everything in your power to reach your full potential.

DELETE YOUR ANTICIPATIONS: Our worldviews shape our experiences, but occasionally those worldviews aren't our own. You probably base at least some of who you are on what other people think of you, like the rest of us. Being the best version of yourself requires becoming aware of a previously unconscious process—the internalization of the ideals of others. To become the person you want to be, you need to have a clear idea in your own mind.

BE PREPARED TO LET GO OF YOUR OLD SELF: When you make up your mind to find your ideal self, you are effectively lifting the bar, both for yourself and the people around you. Although your "old self" will fight against this change out of uncertainty and a fear of the unknown, you must fight the impulse to cling to the familiar in favor of embracing the identity that has been holding you back.

CONTROL YOUR ANXIETY: Fear is a sneaky foe that robs us of bravery and pulls our attention away from the here and now. Conquering your anxieties is an essential part of developing your full potential. If you're feeling worried, jot down a list of the things that are making you nervous. Then, record a rational explanation that is less frightening but still plausible. Feelings may not alter instantly, but the reasoning will be stored in your mind. Checking your worries against reality will eventually become second nature, allowing you to make more rational decisions and give less weight to your worries.

In order to become the finest version of yourself, you need to search internally for insight, and you won't get there by cramming your brain with facts and figures. Your best self should determine your objective. Think of something simple and attainable, like getting more organized or reading more fiction. Creating a concrete objective is a great technique to boost self-assurance and get out of your own head.

Build self-affirming rituals: There is little doubt that the world's top performers in sports, business, and politics have improved upon their already stellar selves. What they all have in common is the excellence-producing routines they've established. They can achieve a self-confident state by using techniques like meditation, priming, and goal visualization. The inclusion of a healthy diet and regular exercise is mandatory. And expressing thankfulness on a daily basis is a big part of that.

Be kind to yourself; achieving your greatest self is all about you, not anyone else. Rather than judging yourself by the standards of others, consider the fact that everyone has a unique route to success. Try to be gentle with yourself if you aren't exactly where you'd ideally be. There's nothing wrong with being at a decision point. Stop wasting time on social media and beating yourself up over a recent loss, and start loving yourself. You need to get out of the house and go for a stroll. Go out and do something you like. Remember to keep your critical inner monologue in check and replace it with encouraging self-talk.

LEARN TO BE YOUR OWN BOSS BY EFFECTIVELY MANAGING YOURSELF: Learning to be your own boss through successful self-management is an important step in becoming the best version of yourself. An efficient use of time reduces anxiety, helps you become more of your best self, and frees you from the pressure of pleasing others. Maintaining accountability and managing your resources effectively requires periodic reviews at the monthly, quarterly, and yearly levels. Self-management makes you a more valuable asset to your team.

CARRY ON A GOOD ATTITUDE: There will be bumps in the road as you discover who you were meant to be. Develop "positive" feelings like curiosity, openness, and enthusiasm instead of pessimism. Think of setbacks not as failures but as opportunities. Staying optimistic can allow you to see novel approaches to problems that you would have overlooked if you allowed yourself to get mired in pessimistic thinking.

One of the Human Needs that must be met for us to experience happiness is to feel that we are making a difference in the world. Volunteering increases feelings of appreciation and prosperity in our own life. One way that people of all backgrounds and identities can be their best selves is by volunteering their time, talents, expertise, or resources. Self-actualization is a lengthy process, and it's easy to get discouraged along the way. To paraphrase an ancient adage, "don't sweat the small stuff" or set impossible goals for yourself. Therefore, even if the process of self-actualization can be intimidating, you shouldn't allow that stop you. Keep an open mind and just take things day by day.

CHAPTER 11

TO BECOME A GOOD BOSS, YOU SHOULD BE YOURSELF THROUGH THE PROCESS

Despite the overused adage that "being yourself" is the key to success, there are genuine risks associated with pretending to be someone else in the business. We lose sight of who we are in favor of becoming someone else, someone better. We might get lost and never find our way back. Many people never take the time to discover who they really are or even try to comprehend themselves. This person allows others to define them. They allowed the expectations of others to shape what they aspired to be in life. It's a convenient way out. Thankfully, you are not like that. It's important to you to find out who you really are on the inside. The world of possibilities and fulfillment awaits you once you do. You may be fooling yourself if you think the person you present to the world is who you really are.

So, what does it mean to be a B.O.S.S. at being oneself? Simply put, authenticity means being who you say you are. Giving your best implies not promising more than you can deliver or trying to change course when you're already content with the status quo. Having integrity means always being as professional as you can be. This involves being honest about your level of knowledge and not trying to pass yourself off as more or less knowledgeable as you actually are. This includes not trying to hide the fact that you're overweight, old, or in a difficult financial situation. To accomplish so requires taking pride in the skills and knowledge you already possess.

To truly be authentic, you must first understand what you value most and then base your daily actions on those priorities. Included in this category are the following actions and attitudes: accepting and celebrating your physical appearance, intelligence, personality, and talents; knowing your likes and dislikes and setting appropriate boundaries; defining your own personal operating system and beliefs; and accepting responsibility for your own choices and actions. figuring out and adhering to your own personal definition of integrity; voicing your own thoughts and beliefs, regardless of what others may say; Taking off your mask, tearing down your walls, and not being so hard on yourself. Time, curiosity, and the willingness to let go of masks are all necessary on the path to self-realization and acceptance.

"Being yourself" implies embracing the unique culture, history, sense of humor, idiosyncrasies, oddities, and conventions that make up your business. Simply put, you get what you see. It's great to sign up for work that will push you beyond your comfort zone, but that doesn't mean you have to bury your true self in the process. Owning your company's unique character and being confident in what people (customers, clients, competitors, and staff) see will allow you to focus on growth rather than maintaining appearances.

Being genuine has the benefit of allowing you to do great things, which is impossible when you put up a false front. You can't even see yourself in the mirror when you're wearing your B.I.T.C.H. mask, which is ironic in and of itself. It's fine to let yourself emotionally and psychologically expire (which may be seen in someone's eyes) as you grow weary of doing nothing of worth, because you never existed to begin with.

Experience has shown me that there are some very bad outcomes to having your community, clients, and competitors not know the "true you": Customers will go, money will be lost, employees will leave, oddball customers and workers who aren't a good fit will be drawn to your business, and you'll be depressed, wondering what the point is.

How then do we arrive at our genuine selves? To what extent can we restore our individuality in a world obsessed with B.I.T.C.H. types who aren't who they say they are? Here are some easy steps you can take to regain your sense of identity.

A Guide to Accepting and Celebrating Your Unique Strengths and Flaws There is no such thing as a flawless human being because we all have flaws and are layered. In spite of our greatest efforts, we will always have our flaws. What sets us apart as human beings and allows us to develop is the combination of our strengths and weaknesses. You are not defined by your defects and weaknesses, but they are an integral part of your unique character. Beginning with accepting oneself fully, flaws and all, is the first step towards finding your true identity. As imperfect as we all are, this is what ultimately unites us as human beings. You shouldn't hide your actual self from yourself (or other people). Admitting that you are not perfect allows you to develop and learn about who you truly are. The secret to realizing our full potential is learning to accept ourselves.

FOCUS ON THE FUTURE, NOT THE PAST: Many of us are stuck in our current selves because we refuse to let go of the habits and mentality that got us here in the first place. Keep in mind that mistakes you've made in the past do not define you. There's more to you than meets the eye. Because of the randomness of life, we all make mistakes from time to time. The chance to discover who you truly are, however, lies in reflecting on and improving upon past decisions and using that knowledge to guide future actions. We can't accept who we are now and grow into in the future if we keep dwelling on our prior selves.

ACT ON YOUR VALUES: Everyone has principles that guide their actions. But if we don't stand up for our principles, then what are they? To truly be yourself, it is essential to fight for your beliefs and conduct your daily life in accordance with your core values. Just because you disagree with someone doesn't mean you have to go to a demonstration or publicly shame them. Furthermore, it does not imply that you should force others to share your morals and convictions. For the sake of pleasing your customers, you should never compromise on your core ideas and ideals.

NOTHING GOOD COMES FROM COMPARING YOURSELF TO OTHERS: In general, people enjoy interacting with others. Humans are social creatures who prosper in groups of all sizes. All of us crave a sense of belonging and approval. Unfortunately, our self-esteem might suffer when we constantly try to conform to the expectations of others. We are always on the lookout for approval from other people because we really want to feel liked and accepted by them. Because of this, many of us try to conceal who we really are out of fear of rejection. As a result of wanting to be liked, we may put on a front that prevents others from ever getting to know the real us. Once you take off the mask and stop trying to measure up to other people's expectations, you'll finally have the confidence to be who you truly are.

CHAPTER 12

TO BECOME A GOOD BOSS, YOU SHOULD FOLLOW YOUR INTUITIVE GUIDE

If you ask the most successful businesspeople, they'll tell you that it's a combination of things—the usual suspects like "hard work, fantastic team, amazing idea, passion, long hours"—but also that they trusted their gut. They were being directed by an internal voice, and they made the decision to follow it. We have numerous names for intuition: gut feeling, quick knowing, inner voice, and instinctual wisdom. Intuition, in its most basic form, is the uncanny awareness of the truth of any given question or circumstance, independent of evidence, rational analysis, or logical deduction. Invisible yet potent intelligence is freely accessible to everyone who wants it. How often do you have a strong intuition that something is about to happen, and then it actually does? Something like knowing exactly when someone is going to call you or anticipating someone else's next words? Intuition, if you will. It can also be crucial in determining the appropriate course of action to take given the circumstances. Incomplete solutions can be found through logic and analysis. Since everyone possesses this natural sixth sense, especially while running a business, there is no need to ignore it. Combining intuition with data may validate company decisions like product development, new hires, and staffing strategies.

Business-related intuition can be relied upon when making crucial choices like where to put money into expansion, which marketing channels will yield the best results, and which customers should be the focus of your efforts. Also, it can help you make decisions about future projects, boost your professional self-assurance, and improve your ability to serve current and potential clients.

You need to rely on your intuition a lot in business. Despite its obvious benefits, this superpower is often overlooked because of its intangibility and seeming absence. If you pay attention to your gut feelings when making business decisions, you'll enhance that ability and be better able to act in ways that ultimately benefit your bottom line. Consider your intuition to be your personal GPS system. Feelings, knowledge, and direct messages are all possible sources of intuition.

Intuition is a skill that can be developed by anyone, however it may take time and effort. As an alternative to seeking external counsel when you are feeling uncertain, overwhelmed, or confused, you can train yourself to go yourself for the solutions. If you're not paying attention, your intuition or inner guide is telling you what to do. To many, the most important thing is to get things done. It's possible that we don't notice the effects of our intuition, but they are unquestionably there. When you pay attention to your gut, you receive valuable information that can guide your choices.

When making important choices, trust your gut. A pain-gain model or a pro/con list immediately come to mind when considering the decision-making tools at our disposal. However, we wouldn't always benefit from viewing the world through such a binary lens. More often than not, we've made countless iterations of a pros and cons list, yet we're still at a loss as to how to proceed with the decision at hand. (Have you been there before?!). If you're having trouble deciding, trusting your gut instinct may assist. It can decide a tie in your list of pros and cons. To determine if something is suitable for you, this is often the simplest approach.

As a business owner, your success depends heavily on your ability to trust and rely on your gut instincts. When you develop the ability to trust your instincts and make snap decisions based on your emotions, it becomes second nature to overcome difficulties. As soon as you have your trusty intuition on your side, you can conquer any obstacle standing in your way. There are many ways in which developing your intuitive abilities can make you a more effective business leader, but ultimately, a more effective business owner means greater profitability for their company.

Be Aware Of How Strong Your Innate Perceptive Abilities Are

The first step in developing your intuitive abilities is becoming aware of how strong they already are. The key is to deliberate about each choice you make as the day progresses. Consider whether you arrive at your conclusions by reason or gut instinct. Small choices like what to eat for breakfast, which TV show to watch, or whether to have coffee or tea in the afternoon all add up over time. Making decisions based on your intuition is a great first step in developing your inner wisdom and providing inspiration to others.

How Can You Use Intuition in Business?

Examine your progress toward your goals and make any necessary adjustments to your mission and vision statements. Using your intuition will help you get in touch with your emotions and verify your true resonances, keeping you inspired and invested in your work. This is a must if you want to make progress in life or in your business.

Analyze the dynamic of the team and figure out the best strategy to get everyone working together. Bringing a team together and getting people to work cohesively can be difficult, but following your gut can help you discover the correct approach. Don't ignore your gut feeling that something is wrong or that some members of the team aren't feeling like they belong, instead use it to make adjustments that will get everyone back into peak performance mode.

Hear the advice of your heart. When we are unsure about what to do, it is our nature to ask for guidance. However, in the end, you are the only one who can truly know who you are. Don't second-guess yourself; you know the solution. It's much simpler to tune in to your intuition when your thoughts are at a minimum. Make time for some quiet introspection or meditation. Feel free to pose any inquiries you may have and take everything under consideration. The answers you seek will find you if you are receptive to them.

Make smart hires to build your business. Did you ever hire someone who seemed perfect on paper, but you could tell right away that something was amiss when they started working for you? Avoid wasting time and money on unqualified applicants any longer. Listen to your gut when something just doesn't seem right. Determine which parts of the organization, if any, will benefit most from outside help in achieving their stated goals.

The answer to everyone else's problems seems so obvious, but we can't seem to "see" it for our own. Intuition can help you 'see' the problems that need to be addressed. You must be receptive to the hints that are constantly being thrown at you. Create or verify the sales, marketing, and other business strategies and plans that will lead to the realization of your organization's goal. You can verify your plans with your intuition. Your chances of coming up with a brilliant company idea significantly increase when you go back to previous concepts and analyze them using intuitive methods.

You need to have faith in yourself to be able to tune into your inner guidance system. This necessitates not ignoring warning signs and instead giving them serious consideration. It also implies an openness to diving headfirst into whatever it is that's calling to you. Even though our intuition seems irrational at the time, developing our ability to believe and follow its guidance is key to success. Keep an open mind and heart to the signs. Recognize your own strength and trust that you can overcome any challenge.

Be mindful and keep an eye on the results of acting on your gut instincts. Take note of the times you rely on your gut instinct. Do not be afraid to say that you have taken a decision that ran counter to your gut instinct. Consider the outcomes, whatever they may be. Which warning indicators did you notice? That one didn't make the cut, did it?

Put an end to thinking in a singular fashion. You can only get so far in business using your head alone. Bring your intuitive abilities together with your logical ones. This is fundamental to advancing your plans, choices, and efficiency.

Insight gained through intuition is priceless. If you make an effort to hone your intuition, I guarantee you'll see a dramatic improvement in your professional and personal life. You can better understand how your intuition is guiding you if you keep a journal of your feelings and daily progress toward your goals.

CHAPTER 13

AUTHENTICITY IS KEY TO BUSINESS LEADERSHIP

To be a leader, you have to be willing to let your true self shine. If you try to replicate the success of another leader, you are doomed to fail. A CEO who puts little of himself into his leadership actions will not inspire loyalty from his staff. Everyone is looking for genuine leaders.

In today's organizations, authenticity is highly sought after but sadly in limited supply due to rising disillusionment with smooth, ersatz, airbrushed leadership. Leaders and followers alike value authenticity because it denotes genuineness, honesty, and moral rectitude. The genuine article; the quality that singles out exceptional leaders.

Authenticity is essential for effective leadership, yet it is often misinterpreted, even by those in leadership positions. That one is born with the trait of authenticity or that one is not is a common misconception. In reality, genuineness is something that other people must perceive in you. No leader can honestly say, "I am authentic," when they look in the mirror. Individuals are incapable of genuineness on their own. What other people think of you—what they perceive as genuine—is mainly under your control. If genuineness were entirely intrinsic, there'd be nothing you could do to cultivate it and, by extension, little you could do to improve your leadership skills.

True, leaders who don't learn to rein in the expression of their true selves quickly find themselves in hot water. Adhering to the maxim "be yourself" is the essence of authenticity. It's about having confidence in one's own identity and speaking truthfully about one's own character. Instead of pretending to be someone you're not, genuine people work to perfect the qualities that make them themselves. There's a lot of merit behind the idea that authenticity is a leadership quality in the corporate world. Leaders are respected and looked to for direction since they establish the standard for the organization. Therefore, business leaders that are able to be honest can build a culture of authenticity inside their organization, which can lead to a number of benefits.

Take Janet, for example. She's a manager at a major North American cosmetics firm. Although Janet had humble beginnings in the workforce as a trainee, his superiors quickly recognized his potential and promoted him. Our HR team was successful in convincing Janet to pursue higher education, and she now holds a respectable degree. They welcomed her back to work with open arms afterward. At the organization, she managed many projects and developed skills as a team leader. Her strengths as a leader were her talents and her candor.

When Janet relocated to the headquarters and began advising the company's top brass, everything began to go apart. Janet was advised by HR to take the new post in order to better prepare herself for a future leadership role in the field. But the headquarters were political, and Janet realized that her husband's forthrightness often fell on deaf ears. She was told she needed to improve her ability to persuade others and that she didn't grasp the complexities of certain circumstances. Janet attempted to soften her forthright manner, but she was never able to match the political sophistication of her superiors. Her sense of direction began to falter. She wavered between indecisiveness and sudden outbursts of fury as she fought to reclaim her former forthrightness while she sought to make sense of office politics. For the first time, she genuinely questioned her own skills. Janet is still employed by the cosmetics firm, but she has no hope of advancing in her current position.

In your professional lives, you have undoubtedly encountered multiple Janets. Her experience exemplifies the challenge leaders' face when trying to communicate their own identities while also accommodating the many identities of the teams they hope to guide. Great leaders stand out from average CEOs because of their ability to strike this balance while being true to themselves. Managing one's own authenticity is a difficult but necessary part of becoming a great leader, as counterintuitive as that may sound.

True authenticity cannot be manufactured. It can't be an act because it so accurately depicts the leader's true nature. However, effective leaders appear to have an innate sense of when and how to convey particular aspects of their personalities to different constituents. They're like chameleons in that they can change to suit the needs of the group they're in charge of without compromising who they are at heart. Authentic leaders have a clear vision of their destination but never lose touch with their roots. Extremely perceptive, they use the intuition honed by formative, often traumatic experiences to comprehend the hopes and fears of the people they hope to persuade. They are still unique people, but they understand how to fit in and even thrive within established social and business cultures, and how to use those cultures as a springboard for revolutionary innovation.

Authenticity in leadership is a two-pronged difficulty. Followers, and especially consumers, will never perceive you as authentic if your words and actions are at odds with one another. Although it is common knowledge that credibility must be earned over time through consistent actions, a truly exceptional leader goes well beyond merely acknowledging the need of authenticity. He'll experience it in real time constantly. It is not an exaggeration to suggest that a great leader is obsessed with living out his ideals.

Your genuineness will shine through in all aspect of your business, from the way you interact with customers to the information you share about the products and services you offer. True authenticity is essential to establishing credibility and attracting customers to your brand.

Benefits of Authenticity in Business

The best business strategy is to be authentic. It is important for leaders to be trustworthy in their dealings with staff, clients, and investors. If people don't trust you, they will see through any pretenses you make and refuse to conduct business with you. We've covered why being genuine is so important for CEOs, and how you can start being more like your true self right now.

In business, being genuine may pay off for a number of reasons. When you're yourself, you increase the likelihood that others will trust you. Establishing trust is crucial in every partnership, be it personal or professional. Moreover, consumers have a preference for brands they believe to be genuine and authentic, so striking this balance is essential to gaining and keeping a loyal following. Additionally, being genuine increases your chances of achieving your goals. People are more likely to back your cause if they have faith in you or what you're doing. Being genuine also aids in maintaining drive and concentration; after all, it's simpler to succeed at something you're enthusiastic about.

Leadership that is genuine may earn the respect of followers at all levels: workers, clients, and investors.

Because of this, followers will respond favorably to a leader who is open and honest with them. Being vulnerable is a part of being genuine, and it can help you form stronger bonds with others. Being genuine helps leaders gain followers' trust, forges new relationships, and exposes their own weaknesses. To excel as a leader, it's important to stay loyal to who you are.

For Business Leaders, Authenticity Is Crucial

Leaders in any field would do well to remember how important it is to be themselves at all times. Being genuine can be challenging, but it's always worthwhile. I think you should give being genuine a shot because the upsides are much greater than any potential downsides. It could turn out to be surprisingly beneficial to your company.

People are more likely to follow a leader who is honest and open with them. This is true of every connection between a leader and their subordinates, customers, or investors. A leader's honesty and authenticity will be appreciated by his or her followers because of the fact that they can tell the difference when someone is being sincere or not.

Having integrity makes you more convincing. If you come across as honest, people are more inclined to take you seriously and consider what you have to say. Once again, this is because your sincerity and conviction will convince them that you are not just attempting to sell them something.

Being genuine helps you form stronger bonds with other people. More people will want to help you and support you if they feel like they know the genuine you. As before, this is because they find you trustworthy and easy to connect with.

Being genuine simplifies everything. You shouldn't feel like you have to hide your true identity behind a mask. People will respond positively if you just be yourself around them. Thus, if you aspire to be a leader in the corporate world, don't be scared to be yourself. As tactics go, it's hard to beat. Simply be yourself, develop genuine connections with people, and you'll find your life becomes simpler. That's what being genuine means, and it could be your ticket to success.

Leaders who aren't being genuine might have a negative impact on the entire organization. Leaders risk having followers who don't respect or identify with them. It can also cause morale issues and increased turnover. People respond favorably when leaders are genuine. Trust in the CEO and a desire to work for the company increase. Staff morale improves and turnover decreases as a result. It's important for a leader in any industry to maintain authenticity. As tactics go, it's hard to beat. Simply be yourself, develop genuine connections with people, and you'll find your life becomes simpler. This is the essence of genuineness. Indeed, it could prove to be the deciding factor in your career's ultimate success.

How to Establish Your Credibility as a Business Leader

You need to have a firm grasp on your identity and core principles. Knowing oneself inside and out will make being genuine a breeze. Being truthful to oneself and one's peers is crucial. People will lose faith in you if they suspect you are being dishonest with them. Don't waste time trying to broaden your appeal by appealing to everyone. Instead, concentrate on connecting with your intended demographic. If you want to make it in business, you need to be a leader who others can trust. To gain people' trust and maintain your own drive, it's important to have a firm grasp on who you are and what you believe in.

CHAPTER 14

LEADERSHIP IS A RESPONSIBILITY: WHO ARE YOU WHEN NO ONE IS LOOKING?

Do you remember your parents warning you to "always do the right thing" when you were younger? This is something I was taught when I was little as well. Consequently, many of us don't give the value of "integrity" a second thought when we enter a workplace and see it prominently displayed on a wall. Having moral rectitude is a must. It is crucial that everyone on the team, regardless of their position or field of expertise, is committed to doing the right thing, even in the absence of supervision, rather than opting for the quicker or simpler option. You can't spend your days as an example and your nights as a deviant, and that's just the way it is. Your values at work will be weakened by your actions outside of work if there is any inconsistency in your character.

Do you intend to better yourself as a person so that you may better lead others? As with every position of authority, leadership comes with duties. Improving oneself Building internal qualities like integrity, devotion, honesty, and loyalty is essential for effective leadership. Nothing can be given if there is nothing to give.

Doing the right thing when no one is watching is part of our leadership duty to our followers. That's one way we may set an example for others to follow. The impact of a B.O.S.S. on her staff is amplified many times more.

The best way to lead is to set a good example. She is an excellent example to her colleagues since she consistently demonstrates the qualities that are prized by her company. To keep your staff focused on doing the right things, you must demonstrate that you are always willing to do so yourself. Establishing a culture of discipline and encouraging honesty among employees begins with leadership.

Integrity is the bedrock of a thriving culture, therefore it's important to keep it in mind while you're making decisions. Not that I'm trying to cause any confusion. We don't need a gazillion laws and regulations spelling out every possible right and wrong (although a good code of ethics is helpful). Leaders should reflect on the example they set in the workplace on a daily basis. If management sets a good example in terms of making ethical choices, then employees will feel encouraged to do the same. Your reputation and brand value will grow if you maintain a consistent track record of doing what is right for the business and the individuals involved, and if you can look yourself in the mirror every day knowing that you did so.

CHAPTER 15

BECOMING YOUR OWN BOSS IS A FORM OF SELF-CARE

Most successful business owners have mastered the art of self-care. You might be wondering how they manage to practice self-care habits while still being involved in the day to-day operations of the company. There is a simple solution: prioritization and efficient use of time. Both of these are necessary if you're going to put into practice the self-care strategies that business owners have found to be so beneficial in keeping them going. Starting or running a business requires constant boundaries between work time and personal time. It's important to remember that taking care of yourself is essential for your mental health as a business owner, no matter how big or minor your responsibilities may be. You'll succeed professionally and personally if you can keep your head stress- and worry-free.

Insights on how to take care of yourself can have a profound impact on your productivity as a business owner. Due to its significance, treating it seriously is a must. It's significant for both expanding your social circle and professional contacts. It's common for business owners to be so preoccupied with running their companies that they neglect their personal health. Techniques for taking care of yourself are crucial, both in and out of the workplace. As an entrepreneur, you need to find ways to maintain a healthy work-life balance. Above all else, you must avoid being too aggressive in your professional dealings. Give yourself some time to relax and rejuvenate. You can't achieve your goals without a sound body and mind, so make taking care of both a top priority. Taking care of yourself is the cornerstone of your enterprise. Take care of your health or all your other efforts will be for naught.

Ways Becoming Your Own Boss Can Be a Form of Self-Care.

Self-Care is a Priority, and You Prioritize It. Self-care is essential, and one of the finest things you can do for yourself is to give yourself some time to do nothing but relax and focus on you. It's a bit comical, but we could all use it. Each day, take some time for yourself to relax and recharge. As a business owner, you have the freedom to spend some of your 168 hours per week doing whatever brings you the most joy, even if meeting deadlines, attending to clients, and caring for loved ones take up the most of your time. Whether you treat yourself to a facial once a month or take a Beyoncé dance break in the conference room (or your living room), it's crucial to take time out of your busy schedule on a regular basis.

Any time of day is good for doing what you love. And certainly it shouldn't have any bearing on professional matters. It might be as simple as taking a few minutes out of your day for meditation, a stroll in the park, a healthy breakfast, or a cup of coffee. Allocating fifteen to thirty minutes to "Me Time" is a good start. This short break will do wonders for your mental state, allowing you to return to work invigorated and prepared to give it your all. Keep your hands from getting sucked back into work by avoiding any and all corners and specifics. If you feel the need, leave your desk. Regain your upbeat disposition immediately.

You are quite cautious about who enters your personal space. Some would-be business owners caught in a 9-to-5 job report feeling frustrated and unsure of what they can do to improve their situation. As an independent contractor, you get to pick and choose the customers you work with, giving you greater control over your professional life and allowing you to find the work that truly makes you happy. Self-care as radical as limiting your exposure to toxic people and maintaining a healthy boundary around your personal space can pay off in ways you never imagined. One of the ways I take care of myself is by strictly enforcing my own personal space. To the greatest extent feasible, I focus my efforts on activities and pursuits that I enjoy and that make me happy. I got a tattoo that says "Do what you love" so that I would be reminded every day to prioritize me when making decisions about how to spend my time. I take on a limited number of jobs at any given time, so please keep that in mind while selecting me. Work consumes the majority of our waking hours, and life is brief. If you're going to spend your time doing something, might as well do something you love.

You must not allow destructive internal dialogue to dictate your story. Truth be told, it may be nerve-wracking to consider starting your own business. Many women dream of starting their own businesses every night, but by morning, they've come up with a thousand and one reasons why they'll never actually do it. Many hopes have been lost due to negative internal dialogue, but this need not be the case for you. Countless people want to start their own businesses, but they are held back by fears of failure and other irrational reasons. If you're serious about starting a business, opening a store, or creating an app, you need to quiet the negative thoughts running through your head. Don't let the problem prevent you from moving forward; instead, try to resolve it.

With a business startup, you may work with other women who have your back and harness the power of your network. The more people you know, the more information you can share, the more people you can influence, the more business resources, insights, and perhaps new clients you can acquire. Join forces and hang out with folks that encourage and inspire you. As an artist and businesswoman who has been in the industry for quite some time, I've had my share of successes and failures; but, I've found that the opportunities to work alongside other women always seem to bring out the best in me.

Service to Others is a Priority for You. Working in Corporate America frequently means our time is not our own, despite the fact that many women wish to pay it forward and serve others. It's true that entrepreneurs invest a great deal of time into starting and building their firms, but they also have the freedom to arrange their schedules in ways that make it possible for them to serve on boards, lead committees, and volunteer for causes that are meaningful to them. To this day, I am in charge of how I use my abilities, and as a result, I get to choose what important to me. Volunteering and leading committees are two things I've always wanted to do more of, but I've never felt like I had enough control over my schedule to make it happen. In my line of work, I get to help people in a really unique and meaningful way because I get to work on projects and with clients that I care deeply about.

You have an insatiable hunger for knowledge. When you're your own boss, it's up to you to handle all of your projects and duties. Even if you have employees, you are likely to be the one who ultimately makes the final call. No matter what the situation, you dedicate yourself wholeheartedly to soaking up as much knowledge as possible from trusted experts who are eager to share their expertise with you. Find as many people as you can who are succeeding in your desired field and talk to them. Don't discount the wisdom of seasoned entrepreneurs and industry professionals. Listen to their advice, as they have first-hand experience with what works and what doesn't.

You promote a grateful mindset. Any business owner, whether they run a cleaning service, an accounting firm, or a medical practice, will attest to the profound gratitude that comes from using their God-given talents to do what they love. Business owners put in long hours and wear many hats, but the satisfaction of doing something you enjoy from the time you get up until you shut down your computer at night makes it all worthwhile. I find the most satisfaction in being my own boss and providing my clients with my full complement of services. You can't put a price on being able to help people and having the satisfaction of knowing your efforts are appreciated.

Building Self-Care into Your Business

When you're the boss, you probably spend your days and nights worrying about the company and its success. Incorporating self-care practices into your daily schedule might help you feel more at ease and refreshed overall.

Just because you're in charge doesn't mean you have to micromanage everything. You've expanded it and staffed it to the point where you don't have to micromanage anymore. It's time to delegate some of your workload when you start missing sleep, getting brain fog, or generally not being able to perform as well as you typically would because of it. Make a list of your responsibilities and prioritize which ones can be delegated to other employees. When you give yourself permission to relax and rejuvenate, you'll have more mental bandwidth to devote to solving pressing business problems and making crucial decisions.

Get some rest and try to relax. Refreshing sleep at the end of a busy day is crucial for the body's ability to recover. Some business owners, however, find the nighttime hours to be the most productive because of the relative quiet. Still others like the opportunity to beat the morning rush and get a head start on the day's work. No matter what time of day you choose to conduct work, though, you should never skimp on sleep. Most people do better when they get between five and eight hours of sleep per night. It's acceptable to nap for a short while if you need to. Lack of sleep can impair your ability to make decisions, manage projects, and lead a team, all of which are crucial to your success as a business owner. This is why quality sleep is consistently ranked as one of the top self-care recommendations for company owners.

Be sure to maintain your fitness and health. As a business owner, one of the most important yet often ignored forms of self-care is maintaining a healthy and physically active lifestyle. There could be logistical or motivational barriers preventing someone from working out. In addition, it is time-consuming to go visit the gym. At the very least, you should set aside 30 minutes a day, which works out to around three to four hours a week, for physical activity. When it's most convenient for you, you can hire a personal trainer or use a cutting-edge at-home exercise system. The Strikingly-built workout site Habit House. The company provides individualized exercise routines to encourage people with hectic schedules to commit to improving their health and fitness.

CHAPTER 16

KEEP LEARNING: AS A BUSINESS OWNER, IT'S ESSENTIAL TO NEVER STOP LEARNING

Being a business owner is a great commitment, as you must plan for the company's long-term success, keep your employees safe, and satisfy your customers. As a result, business owners are typically under a lot of pressure all the time. Being a successful businesswoman is much more than just making money. In today's world, more than ever before, it's crucial to possess the abilities to continuously reinvent oneself. The key is to expect the unexpected without compromising your principles or the character of your organization.

Since you are solely responsible for the company's ultimate success, you should give it your all at all times. Having a growth mindset and a commitment to lifelong learning are two of the most powerful tools you can use to become a B.O.S.S. and advance your firm. As lifelong learners, we should always be pushing ourselves to expand our knowledge and acquire new abilities.

Learning new things is essential if you want to grow as a person and as a business owner. This chapter will explain why it's crucial for you to engage in lifelong learning if you want to succeed as a business owner. As a B.O.S.S., it's important to never stop educating yourself. Making a commitment to learning and improvement over the long term is essential for maintaining relevance, hunger, and motivation. You don't have to go back to school for a master's degree or something like that, but you should keep learning new things from other people, the media, and the world around you.

Making your first sale isn't the end of your education. Or maybe you just heard from your first customer! Lifelong learning is something you can count on doing. That's the charm of it, though! Indefinite growth, discovery, transformation, and innovation are possible at any age. Just because you're invited to events and get to give other women advice as a business owner doesn't imply your work is done. Nothing can be completely known. Continue your education.

How Important Learning Can Be To A B.O.S.S and Their Business

It's no simple task to be a business owner and to keep the firm running smoothly. Actually, running a business probably consumes the majority of your time. Managing the stresses of business ownership can be challenging and demanding. All of this highlights the importance of never losing sight of why you got into business in the first place and nurturing that passion so you can keep working hard and have faith in your company's future. As a business owner, it is essential that you never lose your enthusiasm for your company and the field in which you operate by always expanding your knowledge and skills. Your likelihood of feeling inspired increases the more you educate yourself about your field, read about other company strategies, and discover local breakthroughs. This can assist you keep up the enthusiasm that's vital for the continued well-being and expansion of your organization.

Every business sector experiences continuous change, regardless of the market. Some of the latest developments and recommendations in your field may have already been implemented just a few days ago. Your company's future success or failure may depend heavily on the direction your industry is headed. You need to keep up of industry trends and best practices so that you can predict its future direction with confidence. You can anticipate changes in the market and capitalize on them quickly by studying industry trends.

Creativity and learning are two separate yet essential activities that contribute to the innovation process. Without proper training, it is impossible to spot new business prospects. Keeping your mind open via study allows you to see things from many angles and have a broader understanding of the world. Such a frame of mind, along with the precise information you acquire, might prove quite valuable in the realm of invention. If businesses are serious about fostering an innovative culture, they must encourage their staff to share that commitment to learning and originality. The innovation rate of a company can be significantly increased by prioritizing these ideals and adopting a culture of open communication.

Ideas do not typically just appear out of thin air, but rather, they require careful tending before they can be fully developed. You will be more open to new ideas and ways of thinking if you devote a lot of time to learning and development. The ability to think creatively and come up with novel business strategies is bolstered by exposure to more information and a broader range of perspectives.

No matter how much you enjoy your job, there will inevitably be days when you dread going in to work. However, continuing your education is the best way to maintain your enthusiasm for your profession in the long run. Rekindling your interest in your work will do nothing except guarantee that you never grow bored. Yes, totally immerse yourself in your field. Learn from the best by reading books written by prominent figures, listening to podcasts by industry experts, and keeping up with influential people on social media. You'll be pumped up by all the awesome stuff happening inside of it and find new motivation to produce great work.

It's easy to grow sluggish or bored if you don't put in the effort to learn something new. The question is, "Who wants that?" Not me. By making a habit of learning new things throughout your life, you may find that you become far less prone to stagnation and complacency. Having a strong interest in anything may be energizing and fulfilling, giving you more to look forward to in your professional and personal life.

Sometimes, it may seem as though you have to be "always on" while you're running a business. As a result, you may experience burnout. While most people pursue education for the sake of expanding their horizons and developing new ideas, company owners can also benefit from lowering their risk of burnout by learning new skills. You'll be using a different area of your brain when you take a break from your typical daily schedule to focus on learning and education. As you can see, education is critical to the development of your company. What this means is that it has the potential to be a fantastic, useful way to spend your time that doesn't include the kinds of work that can lead to burnout.

Admittedly, everyone needs a change to spark their imagination, and it's crucial to push yourself by exploring novel contexts, informational avenues, and methodological approaches. Getting too comfortable in your own skin and refusing to try new things will eventually lead to a dearth of inspiration. In addition, you run the risk of developing apathy and carelessness toward your work. One of the most crucial motivators for achieving lasting success being inspired to do great things, yet coming up with ideas lifelong can be challenging without a commitment learning.

To succeed in business, you need to know people, and continuing your education puts you in contact with many people who share your interests. Who knows what the long-term consequences of this will be. You will meet people with similar interests and goals whenever you participate in a professional or academic activity, such as a conference, a class, or a video chat. Everyone you encounter will have something to teach you, whether in the form of novel ideas or a more straightforward lesson in the unique ways in which you and a coworker approach problems. It's also important to remember that being an entrepreneur isn't always a walk in the park in terms of social interaction. It's not easy to get started, especially if you don't have the support of others around you. You don't have access to anything that could provide you with release or comfort, both of which are essential for a variety of reasons. A center of learning and knowledge is, very simply, a terrific location to maintain your sanity.

In other words, if you want to succeed, study those who have already achieved success. Put aside any preconceived notions you may have had about "natural born entrepreneurs." Success requires hard work and dedication, not some intrinsic genius. One can't be an expert in everything, not even if one has all the conventional attributes and characteristics of an entrepreneur. You need to put in the labor and study to have even a tenth of the success of the world's wealthiest business owners. And here's the thing: every single one of those business owners who have achieved phenomenal success has also failed at some point. You may avoid making the same mistakes that plague businesses on a regular basis and end up costing a lot of money if you take the time to learn from the mistakes of others. That's why successful businesspeople in your field should learn from the lessons and experiences of those in other fields.

As a B.O.S.S., you need to come up with your own plan for success that incorporates training, growth, and education to guarantee that leadership learning is a continuous process throughout your entire life. My lifetime of experience and education in coaching CEOs for peak performance informs this proposal. There's no time like the present to make a fresh start and attempt something new, in my opinion. There will always be a solution, so don't give up if your business venture doesn't go as planned. Curiosity about other people's processes can help you maintain mental vitality and broaden your perspective. The ability to change and grow is crucial for every company, and this is especially true for the company's leaders. The most effective means of accomplishing this goal is through education. It's also possible that tomorrow will bring different results from today's methods. Don't become mired down in your own moral convictions. Experiment with greater variety and novelty. In addition, education should be a lifelong pursuit.

CHAPTER 17

TO BECOME A GOOD BOSS, YOU SHOULD BUILD SELF CONFIDENCE AND EXPERTISE

In order to be truly progressive and innovative, one must be willing to try out new ideas. Believing and truly feeling that you have the capacity and capability inside yourself to see it through is essential if you want to positively upset the status quo. You have faith that you can succeed despite the existence of both foreseeable and unforeseeable obstacles. Having faith in yourself is crucial.

H aving confidence can make you a better manager or leader, as well as increase your conflict resolution, communication, job satisfaction, ability to accept constructive criticism, and overall effectiveness in the business world.

Every B.O.S.S. begins with an unwavering belief in her own abilities as a leader. Because if you don't have faith in yourself, your leadership abilities, and your abilities to inspire others, who will? However, many well-known and successful businesspeople may be reluctant to openly admit that they haven't always relied on such rock-solid confidence. Or they may not always feel confident when they are interacting with their executive teams, planning for future growth, speaking with members of the business community, etc.

How to Build Your Self-Confidence as A B.O.S.S

No one is completely confident in their own skills, and everyone experiences bouts of self-doubt now and then. The good news is that everyone can take actionable actions to improve their sense of self-worth and exude the kind of leadership that motivates others to do their best. The following are suggestions for improving your confidence in yourself and your leadership skills so that you avoid becoming a B.I.T.C.H.

Master a specific field: You can differentiate yourself from the competition by becoming an expert in a niche sector of your industry or business in general. Learn not only how to use various tools, but also why they are so useful and how they were previously employed. You can use this information to better anticipate trends and spark new ideas.

Focus on improving rather than trying to achieve perfection: In business, as in life, there is no such thing as perfection. Outstanding effort or remarkable results are two ways to describe the completion of a task. But if you insist on thinking that something isn't finished until it's flawless, you'll waste your time and energy striving for an ideal that doesn't exist.

Instead, set extremely high criteria of perfection for a given effort and do everything in your power to achieve them. Even if it's not flawless, the end outcome will inspire trust in you and your abilities as a leader.

Admit your worries: Even the most self-assured individuals have moments of doubt, dread, and insecurity. Importantly, they do not let their fear stop them. They recognize their apprehensions, carefully assess the situation, and then take appropriate measures. There is always something that makes us feel unsafe or disoriented. To be a confident leader, you don't have to pretend you're not bothered by things that make other people feel uneasy; nevertheless, doing so will undoubtedly boost your morale. It's not that a confident leader doesn't experience dread; it's that he or she recognizes the reality of fear and actively seeks out situations where they can respond to it from a place of strength.

Rely on your own judgment; Loss of self-assurance can manifest as an internal debate about the merits of every choice that you make. There can be no stability for any leader if this voice is allowed to prevail. Keeping track of how often you question your own sanity can help you reduce the "strength" of this inclination and prevent it from becoming a habit. Make a list of your strengths and use them to combat self-doubt. Most importantly, keep in mind that you may change your thought patterns and lessen or even silence the internal critic by keeping an open mind.

Try to be positive: There is always the risk that obstacles and low self-esteem will come from outside sources. It's easy to fall into a pessimistic mindset and lose steam under these circumstances. The key is to shift your mindset so that you can take advantage of the opportunities that seem to have been blocked by the setback. If the constant stream of negative news from the media is getting you down, maybe you might try limiting your exposure to it. Try surrounding yourself with more positive influences, such as uplifting music or cassettes that teach you something. The same holds true for pessimists, those who constantly find fault with everything and everyone around them. These people are stuck in a never-ending cycle of despair, but you don't have to join them. Introduce yourself to ambitious, motivated people. You can't help but catch their (healthy) positive vibes.

Confidence and readiness tend to go hand in hand. Don't fall into the narcissistic trap of "winging it," whether you're giving a presentation to your board of directors or having a difficult talk with a direct report. It's best to be ready for any difficult situation, generally speaking.

When you know you've done everything in your power to prepare for an approaching circumstance, you're more likely to feel confident. The mark of a self-assured leader is the ability to maintain composure and focus on the task at hand. Second, if you know you're going into a position where you'll have to take charge of a conversation or answer challenging questions, you'll be more equipped to help those around you. This is a great method to build your self-assurance and increase your standing in the eyes of others, especially if you manage to shed fresh light on the subject or in any way challenge the status quo. This is an essential quality in a leader, yet one that is often overlooked.

Every leader needs a boost in confidence now and then. Changing one's way of thinking and breaking out of a rut can help one become more confident in oneself and a source of encouragement and motivation for those who may be struggling to achieve their own personal best.

It's possible to feel assured even if you aren't flawless. Nothing in this world is perfect. In reality, no one is perfect, not even those we hold in the highest esteem. We're all flawed and limited in some way. Our progress is stifled by our pursuit of perfection. It's a strategy for making sure we never get anything done by creating goals we'll never reach. If anything, striving for perfection justifies procrastination. We'll never get anything done waiting for ideal conditions, so we might as well start working on them now.

CHAPTER 18

AS AN ENTREPRENEUR AND A B.O.S.S, CONNECT WITH YOUR INNOVATION AND CREATIVITY

All new ideas arise from the fusion of older ones, so the saying goes. Consider the goods you already own and the services for which you pay. Can you tell me a little bit about the background of the goods and services you sell? When people pool their thoughts, they often come up with novel solutions to problems.

Being a creative B.O.S.S. means you can come up with and implement novel solutions, even in the face of structurally complicated or ever-evolving circumstances. When everything around them is changing and there are no clear solutions in sight, these leaders are able to give their teams a sense of direction and focus. It is crucial that you, as a B.O.S.S., respect and enjoy originality. The business world isn't limited to spreadsheets and key performance indicators; as a woman, don't be afraid to think creatively. Nowadays, inventiveness is a valuable commodity. Business success relies on innovation at every level, and women tend to be more in tune with their own creative selves and the creative aspects of life.

When a B.O.S.S. has the ability to inspire their team with their narrative voice and great creative chops, they can unite their organization under a common vision and drive innovation deep into the fabric of how people do their jobs at every level. As a result, everyone in the company has a clearer picture of the company's direction and how they may best contribute to its success. In addition, the ability to think creatively is crucial for firms to thrive in today's volatile market. For instance, after the release of a new product, it is often necessary to use one's imagination to forge a route for ongoing development and improvement. In addition, the ability to think creatively in this situation has been linked to increased speed and flexibility in choosing choices.

As a B.O.S.S., you can enhance your creative capabilities by adopting a few straightforward habits and routines. If you sense even the slightest bit of curiosity, it's important to address it by learning more, therefore I suggest doing just that. After all, the results you get could end up influencing future choices or helping to solve problems. The quality of your creative decision-making can be improved by exposing yourself to other perspectives, which is made possible by expanding your network. This is of paramount significance in today's consumer-centric economy. On the other hand, being open to trying something new can help you find success when you might have otherwise given up. Having a willingness to take measured risks alongside an openness to trying new things is essential to nurturing a creative mentality. Although there is no proven model to follow when shaking up the status quo, the payoff might be substantial if successful.

Embracing creativity as a B.O.S.S. means encouraging more inventiveness throughout the organization. This may be done by leading by example and implementing a few important tactics. Practically speaking, coaching teams into more innovative ways of thinking could be facilitated by the use of regular problem-solving activities and meetings for innovation. Additionally, providing collaborative tools and workplaces may help stimulate the type of communication and idea-sharing associated with creative workforces.

Similarly, a manager's approach to leading his or her team can have a significant impact on the level of innovation inside that group. To this end, a B.O.S.S. should always play to people's strengths and allow different personalities to flourish while encouraging healthy competition, recognizing accomplishments, and celebrating diversity. Employee creativity can be killed by micromanagement, therefore encouraging risk-taking and decisiveness is essential.

Why Is Creativity And Innovation Important?

There is value in being creative for a number of reasons. It not only prevents things from staying the same, but also helps new ideas flourish. The freedom to think creatively allows you to work smarter, not harder, which in turn can boost output and prevent workplace stagnation. While routine and structure are certainly beneficial, they should not be imposed at the expense of innovation and development. The productivity of a company can skyrocket when a culture of creativity and innovation is fostered there.

Taking a fresh look at problems is a sign of flexibility, but it doesn't always entail a radical shift in strategy. To achieve this goal, you might, for instance, create a brand-new product or service, or slightly alter the organizational structure of your operations. Do not dismiss an idea just because it seems small in comparison to the size of the problem at hand. In the business world, change is constant, therefore finding innovative ways to deal with it is essential. The ability to think creatively and independently is highly valued by many successful businesses. This is mainly due to the fact that every field has difficult problems that can only be solved through innovative approaches.

Furthermore, the field of innovation calls for inquisitiveness, speculation, creative thinking, and a willingness to take risks. Creativity in the workplace can help a firm expand and reap the rewards described above. Here, creative thought and curiosity are valued more than the practical aspects of business. Although bold initiatives are supported, there is little in place to guarantee the smooth operation of a company.

How to Encourage Creativity and Innovation

Keeping an open mind is essential in creating a setting that encourages original thought and new approaches to problems. Those who want to be innovative must fight their natural tendencies. Constantly inquire, be receptive to feedback, and don't wait for ideas to fully form before moving forward creatively.

Getting creative often requires stepping outside of your comfort zone. While it's true that you shouldn't take any chances that could bankrupt your company, a healthy dose of risk-taking is essential to the creation of new ideas and the development of your organization. Therefore, it can be really useful if you create a setting in which it is encouraged. Encourage experimentation and new thinking among your staff without fear of punishment for failed ideas. Numerous setbacks ultimately led to some of the most significant breakthroughs in human history. Instead of seeing setbacks as a sign of loss, look at them as a chance to grow and develop your skills for the future.

Innovation thrives in group settings that encourage sharing and discussion. Collaborative efforts toward a goal encourage creative thinking. Get everyone involved in order to do this. For this purpose, it can be useful to hold brainstorming sessions in which everyone shares their thoughts and opinions.

Despite how tempting it may be, telling your staff to "think outside the box" isn't enough to foster true innovation. When you provide your coworkers the means to innovate, they will take advantage of the opportunity. In order to get creative results from your team, it is in your best interest to invest in them. This could mean providing them with money, equipment, or training resources.

If your novel idea isn't yielding fruit after a few months, you might want to give up on it. Some ideas take longer to bear fruit, so you can be missing out if you wait too long. Don't rush to judge success; patience is a key ingredient in the creative process. Permit your team to learn from their mistakes and try new things without worrying about missing a deadline.

The unique perspective that each person brings to the table is one reason why diversity promotes innovation and helps prevent groupthink. Think about putting people on teams that have never worked together before, but who come from a variety of cultural backgrounds. One surefire technique to stimulate creative thinking is to push people outside their usual spheres of operation.

CHAPTER 19

FORGET ABOUT ALL THE CRITICISM, IT IS GOING TO BE THERE. BELIEVE IN WHAT YOU ARE DOING AND YOU WILL SUCCEED

Do snarky remarks or unwelcome criticism ruin your day for you? Yes? You're not alone; many people feel the same way when they're criticized. Realizing your own greatness is an uphill battle in a world that actively works against self-esteem. The term "criticism" is used to describe both positive and negative assessments made using a set of criteria. The way we feel about things changes because of it. Keep negative feedback from spreading your magnificence, though. Refining your skills by way of constructive criticism is another option. Your ability to tolerate criticism, both online and offline, will determine how far you go in your career and in your personal life.

Some people believe that by revealing their aspirations, they would fall prey to cynics and dream-stealers. The average person has a built-in bias toward pessimism. When you decide to take the path less travelled, you'll find yourself surrounded by naysayers who hope to intimidate you into giving up on your goals. The goal of these individuals is to make you so terrified that you retreat. If you want to succeed, you must learn to ignore their pulls. Keep to yourself and let your accomplishments speak for themselves.

To reach your goals, you must first climb. It's a trip of sorts. It's permanent, and it's built on a foundation of undulating, unpredictable ups and downs. Risk, transition, and growth are the bedrock of achievement. Learn how to pick yourself up after setbacks on your quest. In spite of setbacks, you learn to pick yourself up and keep moving forward. Many people set out on their journey with idealistic views of how easy everything will be. One must be able to deal with adversity if they hope to achieve success.

All affluent people had to go through difficult experiences to get where they are today. Struggle is a necessary and inevitable aspect of any genuine pursuit of achievement. The road to success is seldom smooth, but even the darkest tales can have happy endings. Instead of fighting against pain and making the journey harder on yourself, you should just learn to live with it. Every day is a gift of fresh opportunities to begin anew, no matter where you may be. In this life, there will always be some degree of anxiety and doubt. Both will teach you to adapt to its consequences, which will help you succeed even more in the future. There's nothing like a healthy dose of pressure to motivate you to do your best.

The overwhelming majority of the time, the sensation of complete paralysis will accompany you into and out of each new endeavor. The reason for this is that you have self-doubts. The things you know, the choices you've already made, and even your gut feelings can all come into question at various points in your life. This uncertainty makes it hard to decide what to do next. The fear of making a catastrophically bad choice is what causes you to second-guess your actions. Never forget that there are no truly irreparable setbacks, only opportunities for growth in exciting new directions. You have to doubt yourself without letting it team up with procrastination. The combination of uncertainty and procrastination is fatal to progress. Just remember that there is no such thing as wrong while you're on the road. The only bad decision is the one you don't make. You can choose to believe in your ability to stretch and evolve even if you know you will always feel some degree of self-doubt. The journey to victory is fraught with self-doubt. What matters is that you take action in spite of their objections.

There will be times when you feel completely lost and forlorn as you wander through the most aimless parts of your journey. This is when you need to reclaim control of your motivation and stick on to your vision. When you have to push yourself to keep going when you don't feel like it, that tiny voice in your head can become a formidable opponent if you aren't mentally prepared to battle it. Giving up when things get tough is the quickest way to ruin your aspirations. When you're in the thick of things, quitting will keep you in the middle of the pack. People who are successful are those who stick it out and succeed.

There will always be naysayers, and their numbers will grow as your success does. Getting where you want to go requires a lot of hard work and making some tough decisions. Those who believe you owe them more of your time, effort, or energy will find your journey intolerable and the time and effort it requires intolerable. The successful make huge personal sacrifices in order to reach their goals, and they have faith that those destined to accompany them on their path will understand and support them. Those who don't share your idea with the same fervor as you will likely get estranged from you. The road ahead of you will get narrower as you progress; competition for the top spots will increase.

The truth is that people rarely like other people who have achieved great success. Being unique, noticeable, and modestly pursuing one's goals attracts the enmity of those who are less adventurous or less self-assured. People who are less fortunate than themselves tend to resent those who have achieved greater success. It's not easy to overcome envy, especially if you care deeply about the people you feel threatened by. You might have to give up on them. In reality, no matter who you are or what you do, there will always be some individuals who dislike you. You can use these persons and events as motivation and resilience training. The sweetest vengeance is a job well done. Master the art of turning your detractors into motivation.

Taking calculated risks is essential in every endeavor. You have to take a chance by stepping into the unknown. If you want to succeed, you'll have to make risky decisions all the time. The whole idea of taking a chance is terrifying. Either your reputation or your life money could be at risk. You might get called out publicly and made to feel stupid. It's likely that you'll have to pick up the pieces and begin again and again. As with any worthwhile endeavor, getting ahead requires giving up the familiar in favor of the unknown. All you need is a little bit of hope. Both the benefits and the costs might be substantial. The only way to get back up is to experience defeat. The failure of one gamble leads to the success of another, since it forces you to explore new avenues and test your limits. If you want to succeed in the long run, you need to develop the character trait of resilience. The point of failure is to help you hone your approach to future success.

Keep your chin up; you'll see that the effort was well worth it. You can do anything if you maintain an optimistic frame of mind. You need to have faith that your actions are moral. One must have faith in one's own abilities and confidence in the method being employed. You can accomplish anything if you put your mind and body to it. Struggle is only another component of your achievement if you approach it with the appropriate mindset. The first step is being you. When you've found an idea you truly love, fate will force you to pursue it. But you must have a sincere desire for your vision to have global consequences. It's not about the money or the results; it's about the vision. I mean, that's why you're really here, right? To make an impression, to alter the course of events? A person's value is measured by the effect they have on the lives of others. It will all be worthwhile when you can see how your achievements have benefited and impacted the lives of others. Personally, I don't think of "destination" as a physical location. I think finality is more of an emotion than a place to go. It's knowing what it's like to make a significant impact on others and the world at large. A destination like that would make the journey's difficulties worthwhile.

How You Can Handle Criticism without Injuring Your Self-Esteem and Business

Think About Why the Critic Says What They Do Honestly: Due to the fact that no one is faultless, it is important to take criticism in a constructive manner. Reviewing your accomplishments and areas for improvement can help you take constructive criticism in a positive manner. If you're being too loud, someone may ask you to please return to your desk or to please enjoy your tea in silence. There's a chance that your initial reaction to that remark was one of hostility. On the other hand, if you take a more optimistic view, you'll see that the person may be working through some internal conflicts. Therefore, they are not actively working against you personally.

Determine whether the provided feedback is helpful or harmful: Before settling on a course of action, you should weigh a number of considerations. Is the individual providing comments someone you know cares about you, pointing out an area where you may improve, or suggesting next steps? On the other hand, a powerful individual may belittle you or talk about themselves after criticizing your effort. You're being dragged into an ongoing power trip by such a person. Take stock of your loved ones and the motivation behind the criticism before responding. Think of their remark as a chance to engage in conversation, and if you disagree with it, say so. Focus on the Advice Instead of the Attitude. Recognize that the tone and delivery of some people's criticisms may hinder your ability to take them seriously. That's why it's preferable to reply to their remarks instead of engaging with their aggressive tone. Ignore the useless items and pay attention to the helpful advice.

How to Keep Your Cool in the Face of Constructive Criticism: Don't go over the deep end whenever you're subjected to criticism, no matter how malicious it is. As such, you shouldn't respond aggressively to the criticism, or you might come to regret it. However, protect your sense of self-worth at all costs. So demand clarity, and you will notice that most of the comments that were ill-intended will break like rocks under investigation. For this reason, it's usually a good idea to take a moment to collect your thoughts and calm yourself before answering. Thank people who provide feedback you can use. Any time someone takes the time to provide you with helpful criticism, remember that they just want the best for you. Though it may sting to learn your mistakes have been pointed out, try to appreciate their perspective. You should not take any criticism personally. Receiving constructive criticism can elicit strong emotional reactions. They take it as a personal assault on who they really are. Remember that the envy or pride you condemn in others is just an emotion and not who they really are.

Confess Your Guilt and Say Sorry. Apologizing shows that you aren't trying to avoid blame, but rather that you recognize your role in the situation. It also shifts the dynamic from one of competition to one of cooperation. More than that, it puts off the critic's response till a later time. Don't be afraid to share your thoughts about the matter with the critic. Keeping the peace with others is important, but you don't need to bend over backwards to do it. A well-timed, carefully-worded statement can demonstrate your maturity and self-control. Therefore, speak up when you have the chance to be heard, as even unpleasant things can be said kindly.

Smile: Put on a fake grin if you must; it will help you unwind. Smiling is a great way to brighten someone's day and the mood around them. As a result, a friendly expression can help you feel better about yourself and may even encourage the critic to tone down their harsh criticism. Make a plan to improve upon the mentioned points in the constructive criticism. Most detractors will have some valid points, and it's crucial to recognize those. So, whether the feedback is positive or negative, be sure you've taken the lessons to heart. You should write these down and use them as a set of personal growth cheat codes.

If you're deeply immersed in what the other person is saying, you don't need to feel bad about stepping away from the conversation. Don't be afraid to let the other person know that you enjoyed talking to them but that the time isn't right for further discussion. Then feel free to propose a time when you two may pick up where you left off. Taking this extra step will give them more time to think about and evaluate their criticism.

CHAPTER 20

TO BECOME A GOOD BOSS, YOU SHOULD DETERMINE AND SET YOUR PERSONAL GOALS FOR YOUR BUSINESS AND DEFINE YOUR OWN SUCCESS AS AN ENTREPRENEUR

Women often associate the image of a prosperous business owner with plenty of cash and a lavish lifestyle. But as a B.O.S. who is just starting out in business, is massive wealth how you plan to measure your personal success? Many business owners get started in the industry out of a desire to create something new rather than a desire to make a fortune. Making a lot of money is a nice bonus for having such drive and business savvy, but it is not the primary goal. Others, though, see success as achieving a seven-figure income and living a lavish lifestyle. Neither explanation is necessarily wrong, but you must establish your own standards for business success.

When creating a new firm, it is crucial to define your success measures early on. Every decision you make and every step you take while developing a strategy for your organization will be colored by the significance you assign to your goals. If you're a young entrepreneur with dreams of building a global brand worth millions of dollars, your goals will be different from those of a more cautious entrepreneur who's only looking to break even. By setting clear goals from the start, you can avoid building a company whose values run counter to your own personal values and aspirations. It's not necessary to amass a fortune to have success and satisfaction in your career.

Entrepreneurs who are successful at what they do know what they want and need. They know what they want, and they're heading in that direction. Building a successful company and realizing personal goals requires this kind of focused determination. Clearly identify your life and professional goals. Choose your desired level of financial success based on your present and future requirements. Determine the most suitable entrepreneurial endeavor that will allow you to realize your goals while also respecting your values, beliefs, and the constraints you now confront. Make up your mind, give it your all, and go for it to the fullest extent you can.

Factors to Consider When It Comes To Your Entrepreneurial Future

Very few individuals truly enjoy their work; most do it only to make ends meet. The envy of others is well-deserved when it comes to those who truly like what they do for a living. Having something to look forward to every morning on the job is the best feeling in the world. Pursuing professional fulfillment is a worthy goal in itself, regardless of financial rewards. Doing what you love on a regular basis is a surefire way to improve your mental and emotional health in ways that money can't buy.

Contentment with one's financial situation is crucial to the success of any business, notwithstanding the importance of overall job satisfaction. However, the monetary threshold at which success is deemed to have been achieved varies widely across individuals. For one entrepreneur, reaching a point where their annual income exceeds that of their old position would represent a significant achievement. While one entrepreneur may view earning millions as a success, another may never feel complete in their lives. This insatiable desire to get more can lead to frustration and anxiety. I'm curious as to how you feel about cash. To achieve true happiness in life, you should ask yourself how much money you would need.

Contentment with one's way of life is an integral part of determining financial success. For example, you may consider yourself wealthy if you have enough money to take two annual vacations, pay all of your bills on time, save for retirement, put money away for your children's college education, and purchase a comfortable home in a safe area. For another, it means amassing a fortune and luxuriating in a lavish lifestyle. Think about the bare minimum you'll need to support yourself and your desired standard of living, and then set your sights higher from there. Assume it as your yardstick for success.

There are societal and familial expectations regarding one's status and some business owners measure their success by how well they are accepted in their community. When facing the frequently negative preconceptions about entrepreneurship, the need for social acceptability and veneration can be a tremendous motivator for business founders. Going against the grain when it comes to entering highly respected professions can be fraught with difficulty in some countries. Success and satisfaction can be found in proving doubters wrong by building a business that is just as successful and well-respected in a different industry.

Cause-related funding: One measure of success for a select few is whether or not their efforts have improved the state of the globe. To them, making a lot of money is just a means to an end—a means to helping people and the earth. For this group of socially conscious businesspeople, giving back is more than just a hobby. They devote their lives to raising money, creating opportunities, and making a positive impact for the cause that means the most to them. Perhaps it's because of this that you're venturing into business startup. Making a positive impact in the world, be it on people, animals, the environment, or something else, can be a great measure of success.

Determine and Set Your Personal Goals for Your Business

The act of establishing what it is you want to achieve and then planning how to get there is known as goal setting. Business owners would be wise to devote time to goal formulation as part of their preparations. To achieve your goals, you need to do more than just make a decision about what you want to do; you need to take action toward achieving those goals. Many people find difficulty with the second element of this description of goal-setting. They have a clear goal in mind and are ready to put in the effort to achieve it, but they struggle to formulate a strategy to get there.

To achieve one's personal goals, one might use the same formula and methods that are effective for achieving commercial objectives. Plus, if you use the same methods to setting personal objectives, you'll have a much better chance of really accomplishing them. Annually, you should assess your business's progress toward its goals, which should be in harmony with your own long-term objectives. These objectives, along with more granular ones like sales projections, should be written into the company's overall strategic plan. Sessions to assess the year's progress toward the yearly objective could be held every week, every month, or every three months. Taking stock of progress made toward a target is crucial for maintaining motivation and avoiding distractions.

Goal-setting is a process that aids in the selection of a certain path through life. When you have a clear goal in mind, you'll know where to put in the most effort. In addition, you'll be able to identify the potential roadblocks that could derail your efforts. Having both long-term direction and immediate inspiration, goal-setting is invaluable. It helps you maximize your time and resources by directing your efforts toward the most productive areas of learning and living. By establishing milestones and evaluating your progress against them, you can find meaning in what might have seemed like an endless slog before. Confidence in yourself will increase as you see that you are capable of and competent in accomplishing your objectives.

It's important to reflect on the day's successes and set goals for the next day before you turn in for the night. It is a great habit to make a list of things to do the next day before going to bed. The success of your business can be greatly improved by planning each day, whether you do it at night or in the morning. If you want to stay motivated and on track to achieve your goals, it's important to examine them on a regular basis.

Setting attainable goals is crucial. Unrealistic expectations can be imposed on you by a wide variety of sources, including your employment, your parents, the media, and even society at large. A lot of the time, they do this without even considering what you really want. If you don't fully comprehend the challenges you'll face or the extent to which your skill set will need to evolve to reach your desired level of performance, you may set objectives that are unrealistically high.

If you want to succeed, you need to make sure you have concrete targets with dates, times, and monetary amounts. That way, you'll be able to celebrate your success with no doubts about whether or not you've reached your target. Setting priorities is essential while working toward multiple objectives. You can focus on the most crucial objectives and avoid becoming overwhelmed by juggling too many.

When you've accomplished something, give yourself permission to bask in the glow of success for a while. Take some time to reflect on the significance of your success and how it will affect your pursuit of future objectives. Reward yourself suitably if the target was a major one. As a result of this, you will gain the self-assurance you need to succeed. If success came too effortlessly, set a new bar higher. If it took an excessive amount of time to accomplish the objective, try simplifying the following one. Take into account what you've learned and adjust your plans accordingly. Determine whether to establish new objectives with the intention of improving any skill gaps that become apparent despite your success. Remember that your objectives are not just the final destination you're striving to reach, but also the guiding lines on the route that you must stay within.

CHAPTER 21

TO BECOME A GOOD BOSS, YOU SHOULD KEEP A POSITIVE MINDSET

Keeping a positive frame of mind might mean the difference between success and failure in the corporate world. Successful people always maintain an optimistic outlook. Learn some strategies for keeping your spirits up in the face of adversity. Self-employment brings with it a lot of self-doubt. I know that keeping a positive frame of mind in business is crucial, but it's hard not to worry when the phone stops ringing and the inbox stays empty and I start to wonder if all my clients have moved on to someone else. Naturally, this seldom happens, since a day or two later I always get a slew of project requests from clients that keep me busy. The problem is that it's difficult to keep the negative ideas from entering your head when things aren't going as planned. No matter what difficulties you face, you must maintain an optimistic outlook.

If you're self-employed, an entrepreneur, or just striving to get forward in your field, you know how important it is to keep a positive attitude no matter what. A optimistic outlook and repeated assurances to oneself that they will succeed can be a potent weapon in the face of any adversity or self-doubt one may encounter.

Never forget that a defeatist attitude will get in the way of your progress and success. No matter how difficult things are or how many obstacles you encounter, you must always remember that you have what it takes to achieve. Every once in a while, I allow myself to get bogged down by doubts, but ultimately, optimism wins out, and that's why I still consider myself and my profession to be successful.

How to Keep a Positive Mindset in Business

A coach's mindset is one of never letting his squad see him question their ability to succeed, no matter how long the odds are against them or how dire the situation may seem. It is the job of coaches to instill confidence in their players and assure them of victory if they stick to the game plan and trust in themselves. Having this mentality can help you succeed in any occupation. If you want to succeed, you need only convince yourself and people close to you that you can do it, much like a coach would tell his squad not to give up. It is crucial for a coach to never show any sign of uncertainty in front of his players.

Don't let yourself become bogged down by "what ifs"; they're deadly to building a great culture in and around your company. Though it's necessary to think forward occasionally, constantly pondering "what if?" is not a good use of your time. Worrying about everything that could go wrong is a poor mentality and will take you in the wrong direction. You need to keep an optimistic outlook, knowing that all of your efforts will pay off eventually, rather than constantly preparing for the worst case situation, which will just bring more trouble to you and your company. The "what if" game can be fatal.

Remember that you went into business for yourself or went into your chosen sector because you enjoy it, and that should inform your attitude toward work. The quality of my work always seems to go worse when I'm in a bad mood while attempting to get it done. It helps me to step away from my desk every once in a while and remind myself that I enjoy my work and should be grateful for the opportunity to do it professionally. The results of your labors will improve if you are able to maintain a positive attitude. Good things will come to those who have a positive outlook.

Make sure you don't lose your sense of humor; it's one of the best tools for maintaining an optimistic outlook. Whenever you feel yourself getting depressed because of anything that didn't go your way, remind yourself to look for the funny or ironic side of things. It won't fix anything, but it will help you cope with disappointment. To elaborate, if you can have a good belly laugh, you'll have no trouble keeping a positive outlook and getting back to work on your goals. Look for the funny or ironic side of things.

Don't Close Your Brain Down: If you want to succeed as a business owner or executive, you need to keep an open mind. Confining your mind to negative concepts can blind you to solutions that could otherwise have helped. Instead of being hasty to write off novel ideas, practice openness to them and you'll find it far simpler to maintain an optimistic outlook on potential boons. Focus can be limited by negative thinking.

In a same vein, it's crucial that you maintain adaptability in all that you do. Don't be pessimistic and dismiss an alternative strategy; there are likely other routes to success. Instead, keep an open mind and give new ideas a shot; you never know when a fresh perspective and willingness to give anything a shot will lead you to a more efficient and effective solution. Refrain from being dismissive and saying "no" to other possibilities.

Don't sit around and wait for life to happen to you; instead, take the initiative to improve your circumstances. A proactive individual is one who is optimistic and certain that they will discover a solution to their problem. Proactively seeking out possibilities that will further my job goals makes me feel terrific. This is due to my optimistic and positive outlook, which tells me that success is possible with enough effort. Get out there and leave your mark on the world.

You need ambitious objectives to succeed in any field, and you need a positive outlook and confidence in your abilities to reach those goals. Having goals, no matter how high, will help motivate you and compel you to give yourself daily affirmations that you are making progress toward your goals. Positivity is powerful because it keeps you focused on your goals even when they seem impossible. Positive thinkers, according to the scientific community, also tend to have more physical energy. So, if you want to succeed in business, it helps to retain a positive outlook.

To visit Negative Town, one must avoid the trap of assigning blame to others for one's own flaws or failings. Everyone in an organization looks to the leader for guidance and direction. Maybe you didn't do everything you could have to help that employee flourish. Even if it were someone else's fault, pointing it out is a waste of time and energy. Maintain a constructive attitude, forget the incident as soon as possible, and start planning a solution. Avoid focusing on issues and instead seek out answers.

Make a contingency plan: Never lose hope, knowing that everything will work out for the best in the end. Do not start a business or go into self-employment if you lack the self-assurance necessary to believe in your ability to succeed. Make a strategy for when your firm begins to expand rather than worrying about what you'll do if things go wrong. Amazingly, your chances of success will increase if you maintain a positive outlook and make preparations as though you will achieve your goals. In preparation for your company's growth, consider the following steps.

The reality is that self-help alone isn't always Help: When you need assistance beyond what you can provide alone, seek it out and graciously accept it. For instance, HR software solutions like CakeHR's can handle the myriad of nitpicky details that would otherwise annoy and divert you from focusing on what really matters: expanding your business. It's going to be much simpler to maintain optimism and focus on the reasons you started your firm in the first place if you're willing to accept assistance and allow someone else handle the details.

Give some thought to counting your blessings: Give some thought to being grateful once in a while (or better yet, every day). Recognize the blessings in your life and give thanks to the individuals who make them possible. Yes, it's cheesy, but daily affirmations that allow you to take stock of what you have and how lucky you are can keep you in a good frame of mind and motivate you to work hard toward your goals.

Make sure you're managing your company the way you always imagined you would; this doesn't give you license to be a jerk to your employees, but it does suggest that you should act in accordance with your own ideals. Having things go precisely how you want them to goes a long way toward keeping you motivated. When I remind myself that I made the decision to become self-employed so that I could set my own hours and focus on projects that interested me, I feel reassured that I made the right choice. It's counterproductive to dwell on difficulties; instead, focus on how to overcome them, as this will help you maintain a good outlook and make progress.

CHAPTER 22

TO BECOME A GOOD BOSS, YOU SHOULD BE TRANSPARENT

Transparency in leadership is becoming increasingly vital for female entrepreneurs. Organizational and corporate success are both enhanced by open communication. However, not everyone has a firm grasp on the topic, nor does everyone know what it takes to be an honest leader. Leadership that is transparent keeps people informed, shares the good and the bad (but doesn't overshare), and encourages open communication and honest feedback from team members. Nothing that could damage your credibility as a leader should come as a surprise to anyone. Leaders who are transparent do what they want their followers to do, have high standards for themselves, and keep their team members in the loop.

Leading with transparency necessitates the courage to be upfront and honest with your staff members, even if doing so makes you feel exposed. Because of the constant scrutiny from staff, leaders must act in ways that are honest and faithful to the company's core principles. Employees will reward you with their dedication and confidence.

When you're the leader, you have to set the tone for the entire organization, and that includes being open and honest. Having leaders that are open and honest with their staff is becoming increasingly important as it encourages an environment where everyone feels safe to speak their minds and take responsibility for their actions. Transparency in leadership means not hiding information or glossing over problems. Get the word out to everyone on the team so they're prepared for anything may come. Doing so will ensure that your team is ready for any challenges that may arise.

Importance of Transparent Leadership

The level of performance in a business rises when there is open communication and trust between employees. Trustworthy and open relationships can flourish if leaders and their teams prioritize open and regular dialogue. To keep high-performing employees and recruit fresh talent, it is important to build on this foundation of trust, which allows individuals to work together better and aids in the development of the team. If your team thinks you're a trustworthy leader because you're open and honest with them, you'll have their support. They will give their best to the assignment you offer them if you do this. In particular, team members like their work and are not afraid to voice their opinions if they encounter any unforeseen difficulties.

Workers are more likely to stay put in a company with open and honest management. Having a fair system for allocating resources is a must-have for any firm, and it's especially important to those who work there. Long-term employees are common at many huge organizations with open cultures like Netflix, Heineken, etc. They have no plans to quit and want to stay in their current position for as long as feasible. Building stronger relationships in and out of the office is facilitated by leaders who are open and honest. The maximum level of organization may be achieved by firms when transparency is combined with the willingness to accept both success and failure. Employees can now freely and publicly seek help from management without fear of retaliation.

Leadership that is open and honest with their employees also inspires more loyalty from those who work under them. Leaders that are transparent with their teams show appreciation for their workers by actively listening to their suggestions. By demonstrating appreciation for workers' efforts, businesses not only inspire brand loyalty but also gain the support of their workforce through increased employee advocacy. Humanizing leaders and making them more approachable in the eyes of their teams can be accomplished through demonstrating real interest and appreciation. There is a correlation between a leader's level of transparency and the level of support they receive from their team and peers. Therefore, followers are more likely to embrace a leader's critical and instructive criticism. Leaders who can put their attention here are more likely to inspire their staff to give their all at work while also laying the groundwork for long-term growth and prosperity within the organization.

How to Become a More Transparent Leader

To become a more open and honest leader, you'll need to adjust your management style. While it may take some time for these advantages to permeate the entire firm, the effort put in will prove to be well worthwhile.

Integrate openness into company practices: Most workers would want to work with leaders who are honest and open with them. However, many leaders today have difficulty maintaining a consistent approach. They worry that if they are honest, people would view them as less competent leaders. This is simply not accurate. Having personal interactions with their leaders is highly valued. It takes time and effort to build trust with someone. It is essential for leaders to be able to openly convey both positive and negative news if openness is to be implemented effectively. When people are able to talk to one another, listen to one another, and give each other clear, constructive feedback, they foster an atmosphere where pleasant and open conversation can flourish.

Leaders need to be able to model the kind of behavior they hope to see in their teams at work, as well as be transparent about the challenges they face and the lessons they learn. Leaders also need to maintain tabs on how their teams are doing so they can handle any problems and identify areas for improvement. When leaders manage to do this in a positive way, it can help strengthen trust. When executives aren't forthcoming about problems within the company or when their words and actions don't jibe, though, trust begins to erode. It's quite challenging to regain someone's trust once it's been broken.

Strengthen bonds through consistent communication: The frequency with which you check in with your team and commit to one-on-one time with team members is just as important as the content of your conversations, which is why it may help build trust through open and honest discourse. Consistency and paying attention to the details of your employees' lives go a long way toward fostering a culture of trust, which is essential for success in any organization. Regular check-ins and one-on-one communication are the only ways to show employees that you care about them as individuals and have their backs. A weekly ten-minute meeting to find out what staff are up to and how you can assist them goes a long way toward establishing that trust.

Always tell the truth: True, no leader is flawless, but there must be some who are trustworthy. Truthfulness is understood to entail candor and openness. Keeping one's word, honoring one's promises, and delivering on time are all hallmarks of honesty. Be understanding and sympathetic in order to help people accept the truth even if it hurts, and be open to having difficult conversations and hearing people out. Team together and perform standups. Discuss your setbacks openly and honestly. Disclose your next steps.

Don't complicate things when talking to one another: A leader is expected to communicate with a sizable workforce and each individual on their team. A leader's manner of communication influences employees throughout the company. Everyone should be on the same page, thus an open channel of communication is essential.

Maintain transparency and open communication. Leaders are often the target of harsh criticism. If they are honest, they won't brush off constructive criticism from coworkers, even if it makes them feel bad. Allow workers and business associates equal access to any and all feedback mechanisms. And always remember to alter the unfavorable into the favorable. As a result, they will look up to you as a leader. In addition, you increase your odds of fixing issues before they escalate.

Get the word out about your successes and the company's core values to the entire staff. By putting to rest the erroneous belief that someone is slacking off for no good reason, this frame of mind can assist build trust. It's fine to brag about your achievements so long as you're being genuine. Always keep your staff informed. Share your thoughts frequently. Don't forget to thank the staff members that assisted you. Don't hide the bad news.

Collaborative decision-making exemplifies transparency in addition to listening and talking openly. Numerous studies have shown that decisions made with a larger group of individuals participating tend to be more accurate and inspire stronger commitments from those involved. An open leader will know who to consult and how to get people involved in making decisions. Moreover, a successful leader provides their team members with multiple viable alternatives rather than just one, predetermined solution.

Be unafraid of difficulty: many people appear to escape issues rather than attempt to face and solve them. They don't want to announce what they'll do or what they think, especially to their employer. Because of this, interesting concepts risk being forgotten. Some positive change, though, could be brought about by a leader who is not afraid to show his or her true colors. They have no qualms in voicing their ideas to others, even those in authoritative positions. Members of the group discuss problems and offer suggestions for how to address them.

A transparent leader must not overlook the need of attentive listening when communicating. Maintaining eye contact throughout conversations also conveys sincerity. Unfortunately, nobody enjoys receiving terrible news, so it's important to express your condolences when they're shared. It's important that everyone in the group feels like they're being treated fairly. Engage them in conversation not just about work but also about personal matters, such as their needs or professional aspirations. If you're able to establish rapport with your team, they'll see you as a trustworthy and honest leader.

Respect yourself and others will respect you. More than that, they are real people whose efforts, day in and day out, contribute to the growth and success of your business. For this reason, treat everyone you encounter as an equal, regardless of whether you are their employer or not.

To encourage trust among workers, create a setting in which everyone feels safe enough to share their ideas and work together to find solutions. Leaders who succeed provide their teams with the room, freedom, and constructive criticism they need to do their work. However, if a team works in an atmosphere where failure is heavily stigmatized, members may act in ways that hinder the group's performance. Without trust, workers are more likely to be cautious, disengaged, and unwilling to try new things. Leaders should make it easier for staff to take risks. Being adaptable demonstrates confidence in your staff and is appreciated by them.

Instead, put in the time and energy required to create a setting where everyone feels like they have the tools they need to flourish as a team. Provide kids with a risk-free environment in which to discover and learn. All of these things have the potential to boost the company's fortunes, make it more competitive, and entice top employees.

CHAPTER 23

COMMUNICATE CLEARLY AND EFFECTIVELY: YOU WILL BE TAKING SERIOUSLY

If you want your business to last and grow, customer satisfaction must be your top priority. For issues to be resolved rapidly, it is crucial that customer support professionals are able to communicate effectively.

Having a clear line of communication is crucial when dealing with customers. Whether a customer is seeking assistance with a product purchase or is so frustrated that they are ready to abandon the brand, customer service representatives must employ the appropriate techniques to establish a rapport that restores the customer's sense of calm, satisfaction, and trust in the company.

Constantly strive to improve your communication skills with clients, as they are crucial to your success. Speaking clearly, effectively, efficiently, and respectfully are all examples of such abilities. Additionally, when dealing with customers, you should use compassionate listening skills. Possessing first-rate communication abilities is crucial because it demonstrates to them that you get their meaning rather than just their words.

The 3 Communication 'E' Skills You Must Possess

E: EFFECTIVE COMMUNICATION SKILLS

The ability to communicate clearly and effectively with clients is essential. Customers should be able to understand your company's policies, methods, and other facets upon leaving your business. Speaking in a way that is easy to understand provides the customer a positive impression of both you and your business. Customers are less likely to do business with someone who mumbles or has trouble expressing themselves. The last point is that there is no space for error in effective communication. You and the client have an in-depth knowledge of the business or the problem you're solving. Having that level of comprehension on both sides of the transaction is crucial to maintaining a healthy relationship with the customer.

E: EFFICIENTCOMMUNICATION SKILLS

Customers want courteous, speedy responses to their inquiries. Your company's gratitude for their patronage will be evident in this action. If you want to impress your consumer, you need to be able to speak fluently about the issue you're trying to solve. What matters most is not digressing into unrelated topics, but rather getting to the point quickly. As was previously noted, clients expect a quick response. Communicating with consumers in a nice manner is crucial since it shows respect and reflects positively on the company. I think most people have experienced dealing with an unpleasant worker at some point in their lives. It's not exactly the kind of thing that makes you want to patronize that establishment again.

E: EMPATHETIC COMMUNICATION SKILLS

Empathetic listening is a crucial aspect of providing excellent customer service in any setting; it shows the consumer that they are heard and understood. So that the customer feels safe opening up to you, you put yourself in their shoes and refrain from passing judgment. Be sure to make and keep eye contact, nod when it's appropriate, and apologize when necessary. Through attentive listening, you may reassure the consumer that their issue will be resolved successfully. In order to resolve the problem, the consumer must believe that you share their disappointment.

Rules for Effective Customer Service Communication That Will Empower Your Agents and Customers Alike

Customers want to feel like they're dealing with a real person when they contact a company, so agents should tailor the interaction to their needs from the get-go. Customer service representatives should introduce themselves, use the customer's name, and inquire in a genuine tone how they can help. It's important for customers to sense that agents are eager to assist them, so a happy attitude and upbeat delivery on the phone and in writing are crucial to providing individualized service.

Don't say anything bad. Put another way, there is no room for uncertainty or pessimism in the world of customer service. Dissatisfied clients want to hear that their issues can be resolved. Agents who may not know the answers immediately should avoid using language that betrays an incapacity to find a solution or a lack of expertise. Avoiding negative language like "can't" or "don't" and instead offering to "find the solution" are good examples. Disparaging language can cause customers to lose faith in a company and their products.

Deliver in-depth explanations in response to technical inquiries. Agents must be mindful that not every customer will have the same level of technical expertise as they have. Take the case of a consumer who calls a telecom provider about a technical difficulty, or a shopper who has trouble completing their online purchase at a retail outlet's website. When dealing with a technological issue, agents should put their consumers at ease by providing thorough explanations in language they can grasp.

Pay attentive attention and don't break the customer's train of thought. Agents should listen as much as they provide assistance, as customers want to feel heard. Before offering solutions, agents should encourage customers to fully disclose their problems. It's vital to let the client finish their sentence and politely give a solution only when they're ready to hear it; interrupting them shows a lack of respect and empathy for their situation.

Be upbeat and sympathetic in your word choice. Agents that use upbeat language and exude confidence are much more likely to win over their clients. Agents should use affirmative language to interact with consumers, such as "I can," "I will," and "I understand." Restoring trust with customers using words that are comforting, proactive, and sensitive.

Always use the brand's approved language. Using consistent brand words that customers will understand is crucial for efficient customer service communication. Agents' usage of terminology to explain products and services should be consistent with that used in other consumer touchpoints, such as the company's website, mobile app, IVR menu options, and social media pages. Your brand's vocabulary should be consistent across all channels, and your agents should be fluent in the brand's lexicon and utilize it appropriately during service encounters to save time and increase productivity.

Try to be as direct and succinct as possible in your writing. Customers like quick responses that nevertheless address their concerns thoroughly. For this reason, it's important for agents to bear in mind that providing brief and always-relevant verbal and textual communications is an important part of providing excellent customer support. This is especially important when communicating via social media, chat, or SMS, all of which rely on succinct messages. Emails should be the perfect length to provide all the necessary details. Likewise, agents should make an effort to maintain a personal connection with the consumer by speaking to them in a natural, conversational tone across all channels. Adding a personal touch is especially important when communicating through media other than voice calls. Communication strategies that are effective in customer service combine a personable approach with efficient procedures that save customers' time and frustration, which in turn wins their loyalty.

Attend to consumer complaints. It's tempting to brush off criticism, yet doing so might be detrimental to your reputation. Instead of avoiding the issue, tackle it head-on with real interest and an open mind. Customers want to feel like people when they shop. Just answer their queries and fix their problems. Be personable, and take a real interest in their concerns.

As simple as it is to respond to questions and concerns, there are occasions when that isn't enough. Show the customer that their problems are being taken seriously by getting back to them within 24 hours. Having a system in place that is dedicated exclusively to customer service is the finest approach to demonstrate your dedication to your clientele. The best way to keep up with consumer feedback is to actively seek it out and use a predetermined approach and method. Like many other essential business processes, adequate planning and forethought can have a significant impact on the final outcome. One approach to guarantee that customers' issues are dealt with promptly is to outsource customer support to a reputable contact center or an online answering service.

Start a two-way line of communication. Make the most of the interactive features offered by various social media sites to engage with your target audience. Make sure, for instance, that customers who have issues can tweet them to you on Twitter and get a response back in the same thread. If you have any questions or worries, you can have a one-on-one conversation with a friend through Facebook's Messenger service. If you're looking for a way to get your consumers talking and feeling heard, try hosting a Facebook Live Q&A.

Make an effort to understand what is being said. Listening attentively and then reacting suitably to what was heard is a hallmark of active listening. When talking to someone face to face, making eye contact is one of the surest ways to establish rapport and show that you've understood what they're saying. It's important to pay attention, answer quickly, and keep your mind on the topic at hand when having a discussion online. Make sure you thoroughly understand the other person's message before responding. To show you care about the conversation, say something like "I need a moment to think about my response" if you need time to think about what to say.

Make an effort to refrain from interrupting. It's annoying when people interrupt you. Interruption of a speaker is considered rude from a young age on for most of us. That's true especially when dealing with irate or disgruntled individuals. Customer complaints should be heard out and addressed without interruption. Helping a customer more quickly and with less frustration is possible when you listen to their narrative and consider all of the facts they supply.

How to Communicate With Customers on Different Platforms

Different social media platforms and other new avenues of contact with consumers have arisen over the past decade. These channels allow for more candid conversations with clients, but they also increase the number of channels that need to be managed. However, if done right, these channels can greatly enhance interaction with your clientele. Establishing reasonable time frames for replies is an important part of any productive conversation. If you offer a phone number, for instance, make sure that it is active during the appropriate time zone and that someone is available to take calls at that number. Send a pre-programmed email to consumers telling them when they may anticipate a reply. Don't make people wait more than 24 hours for a response if that's what you promised. The first reply confirms receipt of the message and establishes rapport with the customer. If you don't meet those requirements, you could lose a customer.

In addition, make it easy for customers to submit feedback and act on that feedback. Make your consumers feel valued even if they have a complaint about something you are unable (or unwilling) to address. Review sites that aren't directly affiliated with you are a terrific method to get customer feedback, and many of them even let you respond to issues that customers have raised. Customers will quickly lose faith in a company whose leaders are too proud to acknowledge their mistakes. However, if you address consumer complaints in a public forum, you send a message that you are serious about finding solutions and value their input.

Communication with Customers Is Key to the Success or Failure of Any Business

Boosting your company's profitability through better customer communication is essential in today's cynical business climate. Instead than ignoring or minimizing consumer complaints or covering up your own faults, take a proactive and positive approach. Reassure dissatisfied clients that their voices will be heard. Provide clients with real-world fixes wherever possible to reassure them that you're working to resolve their issues.

Reply to consumers as soon as possible. If your company lacks the resources to handle consumer inquiries rapidly, consider contracting with a call center or virtual answering service. Make sure you have a method of communicating with your customers that allows for back-and-forth interaction. One of the best places to do this is on social media, which also provides useful information about your audience that could improve your ability to communicate with them. If you want to keep customers happy and have a strong online presence, you must respond to customer feedback publicly, accept responsibility for any mistakes you make, and provide workable remedies. By imagining things from the customer's perspective, you'll be better able to respond compassionately to their concerns. Businesses may boost client communication, trust, and loyalty by adopting these techniques.

CHAPTER 24

TO BECOME A GOOD BOSS, YOU SHOULD SHOW APPRECIATION FOR HARD WORK AND RESULTS

It's easy to forget about the importance of our teams when we're focused on reaching lofty targets and making significant progress. No matter how hectic or preoccupied you are, I tell business owners, make showing gratitude a daily practice. Not only does expressing appreciation keep morale high and momentum going, it also has a direct bearing on the company's long-term prospects. In this team, everyone gets a say. They may choose how productively they spend their time at work, how hard they work on projects, and how actively they participate, therefore it's only fair that we show our gratitude whenever they invest effort into furthering our aims and objectives. As leaders, we need to be able to switch from a task-oriented perspective to one in which we recognize and value the contributions of every member of the team. To ensure that individuals feel complete when they are at work, it is crucial that we express our gratitude in a variety of ways.

What kind of leaders we are can be inferred from the way we handle our teams. A great leader is able to recognize and reward their team's efforts, which is what separates excellent leaders from great leaders. Being grateful to your customers and collaborators will boost your marketing efforts and make everyone involved happier. This is crucial as it lays the groundwork for the expansion of the company.

The opposite is true: if employees don't feel valued at work, they're less likely to put out their best effort, which in turn will hurt the company's productivity, efficiency, and bottom line. Managers and business owners should reflect on the value they place on their staff. Their treatment of these employees may cause them to say, "Not much."

Employees' true worth and value in any circumstance are acknowledged through genuine expressions of appreciation. Not only should employees, from the security guard to the assembly-line worker to the floor supervisor, be thanked on occasion, but they should see evidence that their contributions are valued on an obsessive level.

Sure-Fire Ways You Can Show Appreciation to Your Team

An expression of gratitude can go a long way toward inspiring your staff. Each successful business should have its own special method of celebrating its achievements. Get your staff involved if you don't already have a system in place for rewarding success. Gather them to discuss fun ideas to mark the occasion. There is a profound effect on morale, relationships, and business culture as a whole when employees have a reason to celebrate both themselves and one another.

Each everyone has their own unique tastes when it comes to being appreciated. If you like a certain form of address, don't assume that everyone else does, too. Collaborators should be known and understood. While some people would rather have a party in their honor, others would rather receive a thoughtful note in the mail. Think it over and differentiate the best and most genuine ways to express your appreciation for someone.

Employee satisfaction should be your first priority because they are your company's most valuable asset and resource. Why not try to entice the best and brightest to join your team? They're sure to stick around and do a great job for you. Many business owners overlook the reality that employee contentment has a tangential effect on company profits. Incentives programs are necessary if you want to boost morale and productivity in the workplace. Do not view your staff as subordinates but rather as potential contributors to the success of the company. As a team, you need to foster an atmosphere that encourages collaboration, because you're all in this together. In an effort to motivate people to work together, it's important to foster an environment where success is celebrated and rewarded. Keeping a firm afloat is no easy feat, but the right team dynamic may turn into a self-reinforcing cycle of improved performance.

Team members are adults and can decide for themselves whether or not to report to work. They have the option of devoting themselves fully to their profession and striving for excellence, or of putting off their responsibilities in favor of mindless social media scrolling and mediocrity. You can actually steer your team toward a particular option, contrary to popular belief. Your team members will know that you appreciate their efforts when you use a platform designed specifically for that purpose.

Do not underestimate the power of public acknowledgment. This wise saying: "A person who feels appreciated will always accomplish more than what is expected," is a great reminder to always go above and beyond. Would you rather your team members feel unloved and unmotivated to go above and beyond what is expected of them, or appreciated and driven to go above and beyond what is expected of them? There are a number of ways to demonstrate your thanks for your team members. Dinners of thanks or awards, personal messages, gift cards, and fun, off-site team-building activities are just a few examples of how to show appreciation to employees.

Remember that showing your appreciation for your staff doesn't require a whole "employee appreciation day." A simple "thank you" or vocal praise can go a long way. Something as simple as a Friday afternoon off or an early clock out is usually welcomed and may do wonders for an employee's state of mind.

An additional upside to rewarding employees could emerge as you roll out the program. In an effort to boost morale, team members should start giving each other more public praise. When employees are encouraged to work together rather than against one another, they are more likely to regularly celebrate each other's successes. Recognition, however, needs to go beyond merely meeting targets. Remember to also provide credit for intangible qualities such as loyalty, optimism, etc. Demonstrating your appreciation for these qualities can motivate your team members to work even harder to achieve them.

Introduce yourself and use everyone's name on the team. Though it may sound elementary, a simple "hello" or "what's up" to each team member and using their name is a terrific approach to show appreciation. In addition, it's a sincere method of fortifying bonds with others. Being acknowledged in this way is a little but meaningful gesture that can go a long way toward improving one's self-esteem.

There are countless low-cost ways to demonstrate appreciation to your team. Provide them with a break, for instance. Recognizing someone's hard work and granting them a break in the afternoon might go a long way toward earning their appreciation. Many employees are looking for employers who truly care about them and their well-being. I also enjoy sprinkling in unexpected gift cards or planning fun, off-the-clock team-building activities for my coworkers and me. Every little bit helps, so don't underestimate the power of a kind deed.

Feedback that is vague and unspecific, such as "excellent job" or "nice work," is useless. Acknowledging someone's achievements effectively calls for details. Explaining why you appreciated something someone accomplished and how it relates to future work is significantly more impactful than simply saying "good job" or "keep it up." This gives folks a lot of encouragement and a confidence boost.

A true B.O.S.S. takes the time to recognize and appreciate those that contribute to their success. All too frequently, employees are treated poorly by their superiors, who either fail to provide them with the information they need to do their jobs effectively or who fail to provide them with any positive reinforcement when they do a good job or when they are recognized for their efforts. Even the most enthusiastic and upbeat workers will eventually wear down under this.

A simple "thank you," either verbally or in a handwritten message, can go a long way toward making employees feel appreciated for a job well done. Writing emails that get the job done is quick and painless, but taking the time to sit down and hand-write a letter or stop by someone's desk is rarely forgotten. A great manager is one who actively seeks out opportunities to compliment team members throughout the workday.

Regularly expressing gratitude to workers may also improve their ability to take constructive criticism in stride, provided that it is delivered in a targeted manner. In an effort to boost morale, it's important to provide both positive and negative comments to staff. Boosted performance, productivity, and profits are just few of the indicators that a company has succeeded in cultivating a culture of appreciation throughout the entire firm.

Why Show Customer Appreciation?

Customer appreciation refers to the practice of expressing thanks to those who have made a purchase from a company. It's a strategy to customer involvement that is consistent and selfless, and that demonstrates your value to customers. There are a variety of ways to do this, from sending out thank-you notes with initial sales to offering special discounts to repeat buyers. Showing appreciation for a customer's business can go a long way toward earning their loyalty. Companies that focus on their customers' needs consistently beat those who don't. One of the simplest ways to strengthen connections with clients and make them feel appreciated is via acts of gratitude.

CONTACT YOUR CUSTOMERS AND SAY "THANK YOU" FOR THEIR PURCHASE by writing and sending a note. It's not hard to send the ideal expression of gratitude. Most customers don't have particularly high standards of appreciation. Demonstrate to your clients that you're a real person, not just a bot. Express your gratitude to them without making it seem like you demand anything in return. Don't try to sell to them and ask them to "share on social media" in the same sentence. Express your sincere appreciation to the consumer on a one-on-one basis for their patronage and confidence in your abilities to deliver. To some extent, that's enough to bond over.

It can be exhausting and appear insincere to individually thank every customer for every order, and as your business expands, it will become hard to handle this task on your own. In light of this, it can be instructive to divide your clientele base into subsets according to your priorities. Including a fancy gift with each purchase, for instance, will quickly drain your marketing budget. However, identifying your most valuable clients and sending them a personalized note along with a branded gift might help you strengthen your relationships with them.

Determine a dependable method to distribute the thank-you gifts, whether you intend to include them in each shipment or only send them out on rare occasions. It need not be automated, but a well-structured procedure will ensure that it occurs. For true moments of joy, you don't need to spend a lot of money. It's important to make it simple for employees to recommend satisfied customers for recognition if you have a team working for you. A Google form or a few hours on a Friday afternoon spent composing cards could do the trick. A culture of gratitude toward clients can be fostered by including the whole company in these happy occasions.

There are numerous post-sale touchpoints that may be used to show appreciation and please clients. Make sure you focus on being sincere, caring, and attentive. Customers and people in general appreciate genuine expressions of gratitude but are turned off by pretense. Gratitude is a powerful emotion that facilitates the development of meaningful relationships and the acquisition of loyal brand champions. Having strong connections with customers might help you set your business apart from rivals.

Pro tip:

Make your customers feel like they're the only ones. Make sure they know how much you appreciate their patronage of your company. This will increase the likelihood that they will do business with you again and tell others about you. Sometimes businesses will go so far as to make a special plaque for their most devoted clients as a token of their appreciation for their continued business. Most consumers will proudly display them at home or at the workplace, giving you further favorable publicity.

A simple "thank you" for their purchase will do wonders for your business' reputation. In reality, I've witnessed many instances where consumers have left a company because they felt they were being ignored, and many experts agree that showing gratitude to customers is crucial to delivering superior service. Showing gratitude to consumers in a thoughtful and individual way can boost brand affinity, customer lifetime value, and customer retention.

CHAPTER 25

TO BECOME A GOOD BOSS, YOU SHOULD SHOW CONCERN FOR OTHERS: BE AN EMPATHIC B.O.S.S

A B.O.S.S. must have empathy, because workers who feel they are cared for at work are more likely to put in long hours and produce great work. They enjoy working there more, have a better outlook, and are more productive as a result. Taking an interest in your subordinates makes you a better manager, but it also benefits your company's bottom line. Few of us consider empathy to be a necessary trait in the professional world. However, empathy is quickly rising to the top of the "soft skills" that business owners require around the world.

As a powerful stress reliever, empathy is a must-have quality. It's a great approach to get closer to your team and foster an environment where everyone feels safe enough to be themselves and take initiative. Using empathy as a tool for sustainability, we can make the world a much nicer place to live and work. It's both a tool and a resource for further education.

Make sure everyone knows what's going on. Leaders have an obligation to ensure their teams have the resources they need to perform their jobs properly, stay abreast of developments inside the company and industry, and keep a bird's-eye view of the work they're performing and its larger goals. Those who have plenty of information to draw from have a greater sense of worth.

Show your worry. Show genuine interest in the person's well-being when they come to you with a problem. Give them any help you think they might need, but avoid interfering with their independence or doubting their capacity to figure things out on their own.

Training empathy and expressing it also within business reality requires an in-depth knowledge of the neurobiology of both the self and the other during social interactions. Building strong relationships takes time and effort, but it is an investment that will pay dividends in the long run. As well as fostering better interactions with customers and other stakeholders, an empathic workplace culture can boost employee comprehension, employee engagement, and the effectiveness of managers. Because of this relational network of mutual trust, businesses are less vulnerable to internal or external "attacks" and are able to do more.

Reasons Why It Pays To Be a More Empathic Boss

This may sound selfless at first, but there are real gains to be had by focusing on the requirements of those closest to us rather than our own assumptions about what they need. As a matter of fact, leaders who put in the effort to learn about their staff can better equip them to overcome obstacles and help their people move forward toward their goals.

A leader with empathy goes above and beyond simple sympathy for those in need. They put their expertise to use in small but significant ways to better their organizations. They carefully weigh the opinions of their staff members with other criteria when making sound judgments. Leadership that takes the time to learn about their staff members and caters to their individual needs can foster a climate of trust that, in turn, improves morale, cooperation, and output by all parties involved.

Those that are sympathetic pay close attention to what you're saying, rather than looking away or checking their phone, demonstrating that they care about what you have to say. As a result of their genuine interest in hearing about the challenges faced by individuals around them, they tend to listen more than they speak, making those they interact with feel valued and understood.

Also, the capacity for empathy provides us with the assurance to accept responsibility for our mistakes without fear of being judged. It inspires bosses to dig deeper into the causes of subpar output. Leaders who can empathize with their staff can better aid those who are struggling. Leaders that are empathetic are able to forge lasting bonds with their teams.

WAYS TO SHOW CONCERN FOR OTHERS

To be an effective leader, you must lay out your intentions for the future of your firm and give your team members specific, attainable objectives to work toward. But what separates merely competent leaders from those who thrive at leading others is the latter group's awareness that they need to pay attention to more than just whether or not their goals are met. Instead, they are committed to the common goal of producing something of value.

Leaders can achieve this by learning each employee's unique motivations and then tying those motivations into the overall mission of the company. For this reason, it is important for managers to solicit feedback from staff by discussing their own ideas and thinking in greater detail. Leaders may influence how their teams feel and behave as well as the methods they use to get the job done if they take the time to get to know their staff.

Recognize and embrace acceptance. People usually want to be heard rather than have their questions answered when they tell you something. If you can, listen without passing judgment. Keep an open mind and make it your top priority to fully comprehend the other person's viewpoint; then, demonstrate your understanding by restating and summarizing their comments. If you're not

sure they want to hear it, don't give them your suggest a solution.

Pay attention. Make it a point, without bein to talk to folks on your team about things that ar related. Find out what they prefer to do in their and what they're enthusiastic about. There's possibility that you'll find common ground.

Strive to become a good listener. Many man just minimal attention to what their employees ha They are more likely to interrupt or p predetermined conclusion to a conversational par to actually listen to what they have to say. In any come across as unfeeling and distant. Never under the importance of listening to your staff.

Be grateful, and act accordingly. One of t touching gestures you can make is to simpl someone for their efforts. Communicate your appr for others' efforts on the team by throwing a party, public shout-out, writing a message, or simply tellin "way to go" in passing.

Make openings available. Finding ways to hel direct reports advance their careers is a terrific appr show them you care about them. Organize lunc learns, give employees access to professional organiz and training possibilities, and connect workers cross-training.

CHAPTER 26

TO BECOME A GOOD BOSS, YOU SHOULD TRANSFORM YOUR BRAND'S CUSTOMER SERVICE

Profitability in business is directly proportional to the level of satisfaction of your customer base. If your customer happiness is low, it's a symptom that your service isn't meeting the needs of your clientele. Each of us has a company or two in mind whose customer service we've found to be deplorable, if not downright startling. After been let down by a company time and time again, you might have decided to take your business elsewhere. In order to maintain a stable and successful operation, customer service is an integral aspect of a brand's delivery to its clientele. It's an opportunity to show how true the brand is to its stated goals and values (or not, as the case may be). Customer service is always crucial, but it's especially vital during times of economic uncertainty.

Most business owners don't get pumped up when talking about customer service, but they should because of the potential for expansion and increased revenue that comes with doing a good job for your customers. To achieve their economic and humanitarian goals, successful companies are obsessively clear on their brand purpose, brand mission, and value proposition, and they view customer service as a fundamental tool that allows them to deliver these values consistently.

It is important to view customer service as part of a larger, more comprehensive customer experience that helps guide your ideal target clients from awareness to consideration to purchase and beyond. You can employ customer service to strengthen brand loyalty in volatile markets, just like large and small companies have done before you.

Benefits of Customer Service to Your Brand

Determining the values you want your brand to represent is crucial to its success. That's provided in various ways, but customer service is a crucial foundation. In the case of many businesses, customer service may be the only point of contact with the company. This is why sound customer service is crucial to the success of any branding effort. That goes beyond only attempting to prevent negative interactions with clients. It's also about using every interaction with customers as a chance to demonstrate your brand's values and remind customers why they choose your company in the first place.

There is no brand for which good customer service doesn't assist boost public opinion, even if you don't think it's crucial to your business's success. That's why it's crucial for every business with a brand. Brand loyalty can be fostered through excellent customer service by helping customers understand and appreciate your value proposition and by empowering them to defend their purchase decision to others.

Customer service is a great platform from which to convey the values of your brand. A brand's goal encompasses many aspects of its operation, from directing its consumer engagement and go-to-market efforts to inspiring its employees. One of the most understated but effective ways to bring your brand's mission to life is through customer service. Customers will know you care about them if your brand mission is crystal clear and your customer service is built around that.

In times of uncertainty, maintaining a consistent level of customer service is essential to delivering on your brand promise. A brand's promise plays a significant role in strengthening the connection between the brand and its intended audience. A brand's claims, however, are rarely put to the test. That's why it's so crucial that the brand holds up under intense scrutiny and criticism. Whatever the current climate may be, that is no reason to abandon your brand's promises. At fact, it is precisely in such circumstances that the ability to rely on a brand promise will likely matter even more to your target customers.

Because of this, it's crucial to always provide decent — and ideally great — customer service, especially during high-pressure and high-uncertainty times. Consistency does not mean maintaining the same quality of service, but rather that what you offer is in line with what clients expect from your brand at any given time. People will evaluate your brand, and the brands in your industry, based on how reliably you uphold your brand promises in the face of adversity and expense, not on how reliably you do so in the face of ease. That's why, before you announce it to the world, you need to be sure your team has the resources and expertise to fulfill the promises made in your brand's promise. When facing the unknown, it helps to learn from brands who have already proven themselves to be reliable in keeping their commitments.

Customer service is the foundation of a timely interaction with customers. Many contemporary brands focus their messaging on the customer experience. As demonstrated by popular tech companies like Amazon and Apple, it may play a crucial role in a company's overall image. The continuous quality of the experience they provide for their customers is a major factor in the success of these digital giants.

In times of disruption, it's possible that the things that make for a five-star customer experience under regular circumstances will fall short. No matter how much or how little adjustment is made, there will always be a customer experience that is just right for the time and place and strengthens the bond between the brand and the customer. The foundation of this type of service experience is the quality of the interaction between the company and its customers. Knowing your customer's desires and needs — even better than they do — and incorporating that knowledge into your customer care strategy will undoubtedly result in increased brand loyalty.

It's not uncommon for brands to make blunders or just lose their advantage over the competition. It's simple to lose customers in uncertain times, when consumers are easily distracted and brand teams often have to work extra hard just to make sure the basics are covered. The variables that contribute to the difficulty of the situation also present an opportunity. To win back clients who have drifted away, a company needs to be able to provide excellent service even when its customers are preoccupied and their competitors are also struggling. Returning clients who have abandoned your brand might be re-engaged in your business through customer service.

KEY THINGS YOU SHOULD AIM FOR TO IMPROVE HOW YOUR BUSINESS FUNCTIONS AND DELIVERS SERVICES TO ITS CUSTOMERS

Do you have an online store? If so, how user-friendly is your website? If so, how user- and editor-friendly is the shopping cart? Can a consumer save their payment and shipping details on your site? Customers should be able to quickly and painlessly complete any purchases they make through your online stores. They should also be made mobile-friendly, as an increasing number of customers are opting to make purchases from their phones.

Delivery & Shipping Do you offer shipping and delivery times that are practical for your company and its clients? Your consumers are the reason your company can stay open and continue to provide the services or products it does. In general, when a customer makes a transaction, they anticipate receiving the item or service they bought quickly. If you want your business to succeed, you need to figure out how to meet, and even exceed, the expectations of your customers. Customers appreciate knowing when their products are being shipped and delivered, and you should make it easy for them to make changes or cancel their orders.

Do your consumers have access to self-service options on your websites, or do they need to contact you directly to complete their requests? Is it simple to locate and comprehend the data they require? Or is it obscure and difficult to implement? Your websites need a frequently asked questions (FAQ) section with search capabilities. Customers have little patience for sites that force them to spend too much time digging for the information they need. They should be able to quickly and easily discover whatever it is they're looking for in whatever self-service interaction they have.

Incentives for Repeat Business Consumers in the modern day crave unique products. Sales increase and brand loyalty soar. Running a loyalty program is the most efficient approach to gather the information you need to provide a customized experience for your customers. Provide your most devoted customers with an unforgettable encounter that is perfectly tailored to their preferences. Take the hypothetical case of a brewery owner. Instead of rewarding loyal customers who spread the word about your business online with free beer delivered straight to their door, why you throw them a curveball by inviting them on a tour of the brewery? You could, alternatively, give them free beer, but you could make the experience more memorable by adding their names and images to the labels. In any situation, your brand's reputation would likely improve thanks to the publicity generated by word-of-mouth advertising on the internet. That's merely an illustration; feel free to choose whichever method you think would be most beneficial to your company.

Confrontation and Complaint Handling: How do you address customer complaints, questions, and requests when they call your business? Do you talk about them and try to fix them, or do you just ignore them? Is there a lengthy delay in getting answers to their messages? If your company is falling short in this area, it has to start making some changes. Upgrade your customer support software, set up a help desk, or, if you lack the resources to do so, consider a cloud help desk service. In order to better serve their customers, they want to reduce the amount of time it takes to respond to their inquiries and enhance how their messages are handled overall.

Returns: Be consistent with your return policy throughout all of your stores, whether virtual and physical. Customers' confidence in your company and motivation to make purchases are both boosted when you make it simple for them to return faulty or undesired products within a certain time limit.

Give your customers the help they need quickly and easily. Consumers today have come to anticipate a prompt and satisfactory answer if they encounter an issue with your products or services or have a query about your brand. Think about it: modern folks don't get much downtime. Thus, even a 30-minute wait for help from customer service might significantly lower satisfaction.

Provide Around-the-Clock Help to Your Customers: Having a dedicated customer support team or department that operates around the clock is essential if you want to provide fast response rates to your customers, especially if you have a large customer base. The most efficient method of providing this kind of service is to employ many client reps and have them work in shifts. If you don't have a sizable budget, one option is to hire remote freelancers to handle customer service. This can be done domestically or internationally.

Provide a Simple, Flexible Refund Policy. Guaranteeing a customer's money back is a smart practice since it inspires confidence in your product or service and your company as a whole. Customers will be more willing to give your goods and services a go if they see less risk in making the purchase overall. However, in the present day, almost many companies have a return policy, so promoting that alone isn't necessarily enough to distinguish out. That's why it's crucial that you simplify your refund policy so that even the typical customer can follow it. Complex legalese is unnecessary and likely to confuse customers, thus it's best avoided. Make use of bullet points to highlight eligibility requirements, and be sure to clearly describe any important dates or options. You should explain your refund policy in clear English on a dedicated landing page or FAQ post, while leaving the legalese and technicalities to your Terms of Service page.

CHAPTER 27

SEEK OUT FEEDBACK AND CONDUCT RESEARCH

Feedback and analysis of the market might help verify the viability of your company. Because knowing what your target audience wants is crucial to your company's success, it's important to check out your rivals' websites and read both favorable and negative feedback about them. You can learn the ins and outs of the rival company by analyzing their strengths and flaws in great detail. When you've identified a competitor's weak spots, you can capitalize on them by filling those voids with your own offering.

Market Research Can Help You Build a Stronger Business

Market research is a vital tool for any entrepreneur who wants to stay ahead of the competition, respond quickly to shifting consumer preferences, and improve the overall performance of their organization. The ability to understand your target market and grow your sales is essential whether you are just getting started or have an established firm.

The majority of businesses are unable to effectively manage their brand. They wonder, "What kind of impression are we giving to our customers?" When compared to similar products, how strong is our brand? If you want to know if your target audience recognizes and appreciates your brand, you can find out with some market research. The way your company is perceived in relation to its rivals. How would you describe the defining features of your brand? Customers' opinions on promotional materials like logos, pamphlets, websites, etc. can be gleaned through surveys. To better understand how consumers perceive a brand, researchers often conduct one-on-one interviews or group discussions. You can ask participants for their thoughts and opinions as you delve deeply into a variety of topics. The findings will be useful for creating brand positioning and enhancing marketing resources.

New market prospects might be found with the use of market research. It's a good way to gauge consumer interest in new offerings and learn which regions would be best for growth. It's possible that you're in search of a suitable place in which to launch a brand new retail establishment. Alternately, perhaps you're thinking about switching up your channel of distribution and want to see how that might affect your clientele.

Discovering whether your product has the proper components and presentation is essential if you are developing a new product or updating an existing one. Before investing heavily in mass manufacturing, your business can benefit from the research that will reveal ways in which your items might be improved.

Ways to Get Consistent (And High Quality) Feedback from Your Customers

One of the most common methods of gathering client feedback is through live chat. It's basic and convenient to use. Live chat is the simplest and most hassle-free way for your customers to get in touch with your support team when they need a quick resolution to an issue. By using it, you may find out the most typical issues your customers experience with the service. Moreover, If customers get the assistance they need from your team via live chat, they are more likely to remain on your website. Therefore, employ live chat as a means of gathering customer comments.

Finding out client opinions via social media is a growing trend. Find out what others think about your business, product, or service by using the most often used of these tools. Popular and widely utilized channels include social media platforms (e.g., Facebook, Twitter, and LinkedIn) and online discussion communities (Reddit, Quora). Communicating with others who will be discussing your product is crucial. Customers will appreciate that you listen to them and consider their feedback. If you need to gather data from social media at scale, you may want to look into social media data collectors like Reddit scraping tools.

Getting client input is simple by having them fill out polls and questionnaires. Numerous samples of surveys and polls can be found online. In most cases, a survey will only require a few minutes of your time. It's much simpler to get client input and data, which can be invaluable for making improvements to the product.

Do you realize that tracking and monitoring your website's actions can yield a wealth of information and insight? Possibly your first thought is, "How is it even possible?" Indeed, that is the case. Customers' (and prospective customers') time on your site can be better targeted once you have a complete picture of how they use it. In addition, the most common difficulties, questions, and desired features can be gleaned from the Frequently Asked Questions (FAQ) section. Making blog entries that are search engine optimized (SEO) for these terms is a fantastic method to increase site visitors.

A consumer feedback group or forum that you create could be quite useful. These sites can facilitate knowledge exchange. It may also be helpful in resolving everyday issues. More importantly, though, you'll be able to anticipate your consumers' wants and needs. Customers might feel more connected to your brand and your mission to improve their work and personal lives by participating in an online community.

Creating a newsletter and sending it out via email is one method of collecting client feedback. Sending out a poll or survey to gather product feedback every so often is a wonderful idea. Likewise, make sure you're responding to all the emails your consumers send you. Keeping in touch with them and lending a hand when problems arise will let you know what's most pressing and where you can make the most progress.

Just ask your consumers what they think. Whether in passing chat, a text message, an email discussion, or out of simple interest. Tell them the truth, show them you care, and offer them the most improved version of your product you can. They'll respect that and be more willing to share their thoughts with you as a result.

CHAPTER 28

YOU HAVE TO PROJECT CONFIDENCE!

B eing self-assured is like the nectar that brings bees to a flower; it attracts others to its bearer. Possessing confidence makes us feel more able to handle anything life throws at us. When we believe in ourselves, we tend to take chances and go after the things we want. Confidence allows us to try again if the first attempt is unsuccessful. When confidence is low, things go in the opposite direction. People with low self-confidence may be less willing to take risks or make new connections. When people experience setbacks, they may be less motivated to attempt again. When people don't believe in themselves, it can prevent them from realizing their greatest potential.

There are numerous methods available for displaying self-assurance. Some things are just habits, like smiling and standing up straight. Some are more about how you come across to others, like having good personal hygiene or speaking effectively. If you don't naturally exude confidence, it's fine to fake it until you make it; just be sure to work on developing genuine self-assurance.

Even the most self-assured among us experience ebbs and flows in our self-assurance. Display some compassion for yourself if you've been shaken in your self-assurance. Try not to be too hard on yourself. To prepare for a similar situation in the future, it is important to reflect on what just transpired and consider what actions might have yielded different results. Share your story with a person who really listens. Focus on your positive qualities and past successes instead. Join the action again!

What Can You Do As A B.O.S.S To Become More Confident?

The truth is that confidence is merely a good mental state, and so any B.O.S.S. may increase their level of confidence with the correct amount of work. Kindness begins with you, so train yourself to be compassionate. Are you expecting too much of yourself? Likely, the vast majority of us can relate to this. It's only natural to strive to perform at your highest level. You shouldn't put unnecessary pressure on yourself either. Raise the bar and push yourself, but keep your feet firmly planted in reality. Readjust your own goals and timelines, and don't be afraid to seek for assistance or allow for some failure along the way. It is expected and even encouraged that you will make some blunders along the way. Always keep in mind that if you never make a mistake, you will never improve.

Gain an objective understanding of who you are. Gaining insight into your leadership abilities can boost your self-assurance, while recognizing your areas for improvement will help you focus your efforts. The only way to get this much-needed level of realism in your self-awareness is to actively seek out and implement feedback. A B.O.S.S. who actively seeks input is also perceived as more self-assured than their peers who don't.

Take comfort in the knowledge that you are not alone in feeling uncertain and fearful; B.O.S.S. All of us are. Confident people have learned the art of "faking it 'til you make it," projecting an air of assurance even while they are actually experiencing crippling anxiety. Take a big breath, act confident, decide, and take action even though nerves are making your stomach feel like it may explode.

To get things done, make decisions, and take on responsibilities, a B.O.S.S. must have faith in her team members. You should step in and provide direction when things go wrong or seem to be moving in the wrong direction, with an eye on getting tangible results and setting concrete objectives that will help your team members develop their abilities. And be sure to tell them and the world when they accomplish something great. One of the simplest methods to boost your self-esteem is to make it a habit of noticing and celebrating the successes of those around you. Your self-assurance will fluctuate, both rising and falling. Make use of your past successes when facing adversity.

CHAPTER 29

BE TENACIOUS

The key to success as an entrepreneur is a tenacious, determined personality. Getting started in certain fields as a woman might be challenging. It's common knowledge that females, in general, are hardy by nature. We may use that strength to guarantee that we won't accept defeat and will keep trying until we find the solution. This determination helps us achieve our goals and serves as an inspiration to the rest of the team, resulting in high levels of innovation and output.

One of the most essential qualities of a successful entrepreneur is tenacity. Tenacity is often the deciding factor between success and failure, even more so than initial investment, the quality of your product, or the ability to pinpoint your perfect market.

In order to achieve success as an entrepreneur, you must make the choice to persist, and then keep making that choice over and over again. This concept emphasizes the importance of viewing success as a journey rather than a destination. Results are important in business, but because they may be affected but not guaranteed, successful business owners should focus on the process rather than the end product.

Tenacity is the unstoppable combination of resolve, fortitude, and guts. It's the quality that separates a B.O.S.S. and her team from just getting by to actually excelling in their field. Some women have more perseverance than others, and that's what makes all the difference. But hope and confidence in one's own abilities must serve as fuel for one's persistence. When the odds are stacked against you, tenacity is the belief that you can still succeed. The finest business owners share many traits, including a strong work ethic, the ability to set and achieve goals, and an understanding of their own abilities and limitations. Without tenacity, though, all those other attributes are for naught, because without it you cannot forge ahead fearlessly toward your goals in the face of criticism, hurdles, and failures. Consistent effort and perseverance are crucial to achieving any goal.

Stay Tenacious When the Going Gets Tough

If you don't have a clear goal in sight, it's tough to maintain your focus and dedication. Ease your own burden by establishing well-defined objectives (special emphasis on the "clear" and "specific" parts). Goals that aren't clearly defined aren't likely to have much of an effect on the bottom line.

Engage in healthy rivalry with others. You'll have rivals in your industry whether or not you welcome them. That's good news since it means you can always draw on the extra motivation it provides. Take advantage of the human tendency to perform better when compared to a rival. In the event that a rival makes a mistake, it is important to study not only the error but also how they dealt with it and the results. So, how did their clients react? Is there an alternative approach you would take?

Keeping tabs on the competition is a great way to keep yourself from getting too comfortable and to generate some new ideas. Follow the lead of your rivals by subscribing to their newsletters, connecting with them on social media, and creating Google Alerts for their company names and products. Even if you have a healthy amount of respect for some of your rivals, you should never let it affect your decision-making. Always consider how applicable their ideas would be to your company before taking any inspiration from them.

CHAPTER 30

WORK TO FIND YOUR VOICE

As a businesswoman, it can be challenging to discover your voice, but it's essential that you strike a balance between confidence and honesty. I can think of occasions when I shrank down and became quite insignificant, or when I played the female part, and I remember feeling neither good about this nor empowered by it. In the early stages of your new position as a B.O.S.S., it's important to figure out how you want to lead and what kind of leadership style best suits you. Simply be yourself and don't worry about fitting in.

Put yourself in the company of the dogged. Constant optimism and drive are exhausting to maintain, but finding like-minded people to hang out with might make it easier. If you're feeling down on your luck, surrounding yourself with hard workers can help you get back on track. Attending a meetup is a fantastic way to connect with individuals who share your interests and gain valuable insight and support. Consider the folks you spend the most time with. Is there always someone who seems enthusiastic and ready to get to work? Learn about their motivations, methods of maintaining focus, and sources of creative insight. As you can see, the world is full of dogged individuals. Friends, neighbors, and others living in this century aren't the only ones to whom you can reach out. Blogs, websites, historical personalities, speeches, and numerous more sources can all serve as entry points to the inspiring stories of persevering people from all corners of the globe and throughout history.

Sometimes our largest obstacle to success is the worry that we might fail. Don't try to ignore your fear or push it away, but instead welcome it with open arms. Because if you let your fears fester, they will at best be a major hindrance to your focus and at worst completely destroy your will to succeed. Investigate what you think is stopping you, and ask yourself if your worries are warranted. You'll find that most of the time it isn't. Few things are as effective as journaling when you need some perspective. Write down your feelings and thoughts for a moment. Just letting your feelings out will help you see that everything will be fine. Accept that your first few attempts may not be very pretty instead of worrying that you may make a mistake. If you give yourself permission to make mistakes, you'll be far more inclined to take risks and put yourself in a position to learn and develop.

CHAPTER 31

BE A CALCULATED RISK TAKER

Multiple business owners have taken calculated risks to establish themselves as industry leaders. However, just because you're willing to take some chances in business doesn't imply you should expect instant success. However, overcoming hazards takes forethought and a methodical approach.

A calculated risk is one in which the potential for loss is weighed against other factors, such as the potential for gain. Careful cost-benefit analysis is required when deciding whether or not to take a risk. Although it is more common to use the term "calculated risk" in reference to commercial risks, it is also possible to apply the concept to one's own life. Everyone, from the ambitious businessman to the giddy teenager with a major crush, assumes some degree of danger.

The term "risk" is used to describe any decision that requires you to step outside of your safety zone and exposes you to potential loss (financial, emotional, or otherwise). You are taking calculated risk if, after considering all of your options, you decide that the potential rewards from pursuing them are worth the risk.

If you're making a major business choice, it's usually OK to second-guess yourself and get input from colleagues. By avoiding rash, ill-considered choices, you can protect your business from needless danger. As a rule, women have a more sober outlook on potential threats.

It's important to accept the reality of taking certain calculated risks before even putting pen to paper on a company plan. The truth is that most business owners have to risk some of their own money or possessions in order to get their businesses off the ground. A great reward may be waiting for you if you can overcome the anxiety that comes with taking such a chance. Investing in things like personnel, physical space, and prototypes lays the groundwork for the expansion your business will need to thrive in the future.

Taking calculated risks is vital for any organization, no matter its size, location, scope, or focus (B2B or B2C). Companies like Facebook, Google, Apple, Virgin, and many more did not become successful without taking some calculated risks. They have taken numerous substantial chances, questioned established norms, and persisted despite setbacks.

How to Grow Your Risk Tolerance to Achieve More

Get Educated About Your Goals. It's important to do your homework, but you also need to know when to move on. Too many of the clients I've worked with are so prepared that they might easily be the world's smartest expert in their field. It's easy to let the excuse of needing to "do just a bit more research" prevent you from acting. Therefore, it is recommended that you conduct study and make use of the other suggestions to assist you put your findings into practice.

A notion must have occurred to you before you acted. When you take this into account, you'll see that you need solid plans in place before you attempt any kind of risk. Such innovations will be thrilling and transformative; they will also be effective and propel my career forward. How would you characterize the end product of your idea in your own words? But where is the proof that they are negative if you've noticed that? Develop a firm basis for success by avoiding negative self-talk such as "it won't work," "what if I fail," "it's not done like that," or "I will end up looking stupid," and instead focusing on the truths.

Tips for Taking Calculated Risks

When launching a new product or business, entrepreneurs create a strategy that includes a breakdown of the expected costs and the personal risks that will be involved, such as leaving a secure career or moving across the country. The next step is to weigh the potential benefits against the potential drawbacks in order to decide if the venture is worth pursuing. A risk's potential reward is considered alongside its potential downside, and the decision to take the risk is made based on this calculation.

Risk-takers who know when to act and when to sit on their hands are common in the corporate world. These individuals are not deterred by the prospect of failure or by their lack of decision-making skills. Despite the fact that most CEOs understandably avoid unnecessary danger, no one is so risk-averse that they never take any. Truth be told, not everyone has what it takes to be an entrepreneur; those who find the most success usually strike a good mix between being cautious and taking initiative. Maintaining a healthy equilibrium between the two is a crucial mentality for every entrepreneur.

Always be sure you have all the information you need before making a final call. Taking calculated risks requires knowing as much as possible about the potential consequences of your actions. This will allow you to spot warning signs and potential problems in advance, giving you more time to find solutions or at least prepare for them.

The key to being a successful risk taker is knowing what mistakes you might make before you do them. Don't forget to consider any and all negative outcomes along with the positive ones. Examples of calculated risk can be found in all walks of life, including the financial, mental, and emotional. Think about how your company would fare if the deal fell through and you lost money. If a partnership fails, what steps should be taken? How do you plan on completing the project on time if team members are experiencing difficulties? Asking yourself such questions can you in evaluating potential adverse outcomes, from which you can formulate a strategy for dealing with them.

Taking a chance is done so as to advance towards a target. Put yourself in a position to succeed by pushing yourself outside of your usual habits and routines. Anything from finalizing a new contract to growing your company is possible. However, keep in mind that it may take a while (months or even years) to accomplish your objective. How can you maintain your enthusiasm from the very first step right through to the very last? It will be helpful to have carefully evaluated milestones to refer to at this point. Setting intermediate milestones is just as critical as establishing long-term targets.

CHAPTER 32

BE A COLLABORATOR

Collaborating as a business means working with others to share resources, brainstorm ideas, and reach shared objectives. When people are able to communicate with one another in a way that is open, honest, and results in mutual growth, they establish the kind of collaboration that benefits everyone involved. Women company owners, in general, are collaborative and open to new ideas. Women generally recognize the benefits of a second pair of hands in the kitchen.

Collaborating has been the key to the success of numerous multimillion dollar companies. In our world, connections matter more than knowledge. This manual will show you the ropes of working with others. Going it alone can be the quickest option. Go together if you want to get anywhere far. Businesses of all sizes and types often achieve success via cooperative efforts. The ability to work together effectively is crucial in the entrepreneurial world. Some of the most powerful companies in the world see commercial partnerships and collaborations as a way to gain an edge in the market, and they are signing formal, long-term agreements or working together on one-off projects as a result. No matter what kind of business partnership you're searching for, teaming up with another firm can help you expand your operations and gain access to valuable resources and expertise. Your professional standing will improve if you are able to work well with others. If your company is ready to take off, it can help you smash through previously unattainable earnings ceilings.

Finding a Business to Collaborate With

For certain businesses, the best possible partner may be instantly apparent. It may take some strategic planning on the side of others, though, to identify suitable collaborators. Regardless, there are a number of essential factors to think about while searching for a company to partner with.

Collaboration fails if individual companies have distinct goals for the venture. All participants must share a common understanding from the outset. The path toward that final goal should be the basis for all business choices and adjustments. If your working styles are drastically different, collaboration will be challenging. If your possible partners have a strict hierarchical structure but you don't, for instance, you can find it difficult to work with them.

Having a shared worldview can help reduce tension and offer up new avenues for growth and creativity. Therefore, if the members of the group share the same corporate ethics, they will be able to work together more effectively. Using your partners' expertise and resources to your advantage is one of the most rewarding aspects of working together. This partnership may encounter practical challenges if these do not coincide.

Sharing tasks and ideas is the essence of collaboration. And for that to work, there has to be confidence and respect between you. An inequitable distribution is likely to cause discord and result in under-contribution. Not anything that helps make a relationship work. Integration is facilitated by open lines of communication. Having the correct communication tools in place is vital when working toward a common objective with a group that includes representatives from multiple companies.

What Makes Effective Collaboration?

Workload distribution may not be completely fair. Take, for instance, a photo shoot for a magazine. If you're in charge of the shoot's aesthetic direction, you'll have more tasks to complete than the studio itself. You're really simply paying them to let you use their property. However, for this project to succeed, it is necessary that all parties engaged have some kind of fundamental requirement met. Do you recall the middle school group projects you worked on? Someone in the group would always be slacker and make things tougher for everyone else. When one partner in a cooperation isn't putting up as much effort, it becomes apparent.

A competent team player is able to compromise when necessary. Disagreements and compatibility issues are common in relationships. Finding a compromise that satisfies all parties is the real challenge here.

In a productive partnership, everyone wins. Having different people working on different parts of the project will never result in a successful outcome. If done correctly, working together in business can provide incredible results. An atmosphere of belonging can be established through the promotion of teamwork. Strengthening ties with partners and the business community can spark original thinking. When you have people on your side, it's much easier to grow your company.

Reasons You Should Care About Collaboration in Your Small Business

Learning from one another is a major perk of working together. In fact, you can learn something from everyone you meet outside of your inner circle. When two experts with very different backgrounds and viewpoints work together, amazing things can happen. You may count on being in a situation rich with educational possibilities whenever this occurs to you.

Sharing ideas, dividing up tasks, and chipping in on costs are all common features of collaborative relationships. Your budget can be doubled while your costs are cut in half through a joint development and marketing effort with another company. Assuming everyone has skin in the game and wants to see the cooperation succeed, you can be confident that you will get more done in less time and with fewer resources than you would working alone. A corporation might co-market their presence at a trade show by sharing exhibit space with a complimentary partner. This can increase the amount of people that stop by the booth and provide them access to extra tools to improve their time there.

Working together will motivate you. When running your business on a daily basis, it's easy to become stuck in a rut and forget that there may be more efficient ways of doing things, fresh approaches you haven't tried, and innovative resources that could help you save time and money. Getting some distance from your thoughts is important for a number of reasons, including stimulating your imagination, evaluating incoming information objectively, and providing necessary context. Exploring new forms of collaboration can provide fresh inspiration and new perspectives on everyday life.

Most successful business owners value networking and expanding their professional networks. The ability to network and develop partnerships is crucial to achieving professional success. Keeping in constant contact and making sales to the same people could be disastrous for your company, so try to picture the results. Even if your initial contact with someone doesn't lead to a fruitful cooperation, you are still increasing your network by reaching out to them.

Working together, we can solve any issue. Crowdsourcing has become common because of the undeniable strength in numbers. When one person is unable to complete a task, it is possible that two, three, or even more persons working together could succeed. Let's say you're running a firm, and you're trying to remember the most recent challenging situation you experienced. Most of us instantly seek out a partner, mentor, or other reliable resource when we hit a roadblock so that we may bounce ideas off of them and figure out how to proceed. The more challenging the issue, the more valuable an outside perspective can be.

CHAPTER 33

THE UNIVERSAL B.O.S.S. LADY

"You can be an absolute woman and also be smart and tough and not lose your femininity."

~ *Priyanka Chopra*

Being a B.O.S.S. is about doing more than talking. It is about walking the walk. Stepping into your own version of leadership. Your business can only go so far without B.O.S.S.ing up. People will say you changed, act differently, act too well and so much more but that just means you are doing something right. You cannot dim your light for others. You chose to run a business and acting as such is something to be expected and commended. If you are the same person you were before you started your own business, you should take some time for self-reflection and ask yourself are you operating as a B.I.T.C.H. or B.O.S.S.?

If the only thing you have to show for your business success is better clothes and new cars, you are not being a B.O.S.S. Designer bags and clothes, but no systems, employees, processes, and procedures just show customers you are an imposter. You own a successful business, but you are not a B.O.S.S. Level up in real life so you don't have to pretend. Your business is your baby, and just like your parenting, you can't look like a million dollars and have your kids walking around with holes in their clothes and too small shoes, can you and you can't let them fight their siblings or yell at you.

Learning to manage conflict is crucial to any business owner but especially women because no matter how you respond it will be critiqued so you have to make it count. Know the difference between cognitive conflict, which derives from a difference in understanding conflict and affective conflict which is caused by differences in personalities and relationships, you want to know what kind of conflict you are in when you are dealing with it in your business. It is important you acknowledge the conflict, identify the underlying issue, listen, respond, and resolve. Communication is all about creating shared meaning and by the end of any conflict you should be able to establish shared meaning with customers and employees.

To be a B.O.S.S. you have to know what you look like as a successful leader and be vision focused. To be vision focused you have to be very clear on your vision. You will be thrown all kinds of curve balls, but it is your job as a leader to always stay focused on the vision and know when you need to pivot vs when you want to pivot. You have to be the CEO and the manager. Without high level leadership, it is impossible to grow your business, without managerial skills it is impossible to make it happen or make it sustainable. You can't prevent a ship from sinking if the captain isn't educated on what it takes to keep it afloat.

Management is doing things right; High level leadership is doing the right things. You don't need to wait until you have employees to start leading, you need to start right now!!! You have to captain your business and guide it from day one along with your customers. You need to be able to wear many hats and still remember you are a B.O.S.S. Regardless of your primary leadership style a few skills are universally important for all B.O.S.S. women:

- Effective Communication
- Conflict Management
- Self-Awareness
- Self-Management
- Problem Solving my
- Active Listening
- Adaptability
- Driven
- Agility
- Good Decision Making
- People Management
- Confidence
- Integrity
- Responsibility
- Organization
- Vision

There are several other traits you need but we covered the most important. It is not one or the other either, you will need all of these skills to operate in your B.O.S.S. mode. As a leader you are responsible for establishing and maintaining a collective culture and business identity for customers and employees, in order to do that you have to have an identity. You have to create a solid foundation for your business in order for customers and eventually employees to feel a part of a business/leadership they value and trust. Great leadership equals great culture; leadership is not at all about control it is about influencing, supporting, encouraging, liberating, and evolving. Some of you reading this book have more natural leadership skills because of your experiences in life but others will have to learn the skills and that is ok. Leadership skills can be fine-tuned, refined, and then applied in B.O.S.S. fashion. If you are willing to do the work, you are capable of being a good leader.

For complimentary B.O.S.S. resources related to this book visit www.bitchorboss.org

Made in the USA
Columbia, SC
03 July 2024

38045156R10126